RISKY PLEASURES?

This book is dedicated to fun-loving women

Risky Pleasures?
Club Cultures and Feminine Identities

FIONA HUTTON
Victoria University of Wellington, New Zealand

Routledge
Taylor & Francis Group

LONDON AND NEW YORK

First published 2006 by Ashgate Publishing

2 Park Square, Milton Park, Abingdon, Oxon OX14 4RN
711 Third Avenue, New York, NY 10017, USA

Routledge is an imprint of the Taylor & Francis Group, an informa business

First issued in paperback 2016

British Library Cataloguing in Publication Data
Hutton, Fiona
   Risky pleasures? : club cultures and feminine identities
   1. Women - Identity 2. Subculture 3. Nightclubs
   I. Title
   305.4

Library of Congress Cataloging-in-Publication Data
Hutton, Fiona, 1969-
   Risky pleasures? : club cultures and feminine identities / by Fiona Hutton.
     p. cm.
   Includes bibliographical references and index.
   ISBN-13: 978-0-7546-4424-8
   ISBN-10: 0-7546-4424-3
   1. Women--England--Manchester--Social life and customs--21st century. 2. Young women--England--Manchester--Social life and customs. 3. Young women--Recreation--England--Manchester. 4. Nightclubs--England--Manchester. 5. Subculture--England--Manchester. 6. Young women--Drug use--England--Manchester. 7. Women--England--Manchester--Identity. 8. Manchester (England)--Social life and customs--21st century.
   I. Title.

HQ1600.M4H88 2006
305.242'20942733--dc22

                                       2006017130

ISBN 978-0-7546-4424-8 (hbk)
ISBN 978-1-138-25912-6 (pbk)

Transferred to Digital Printing 2014

Contents

Acknowledgements

I would like to thank Ashgate Publishing Limited for their endorsement of this book, and all the staff who, with lots of patience, helped me to get the final manuscript right.

To all those women (and one man!) who agreed to be interviewees for the research that this book is based on, I offer a heartfelt and enormous 'thank you'. You told your happy and sad stories with humour, frankness, dignity and passion.

Thank you to Jenny Ryan with whom this all started, who offered me advice, support, friendship and who made me give my best work when I doubted I could. Thank you to Sheila Whiteley for her comments and suggestions about how to go about getting published. Thanks go to all the 'gang' at MMU; Rob, Jo, Sian, Mark, Helen and Liz who discussed, suggested, supported and picked up the pieces at various times throughout teaching, research and book development. Thanks to Lizzy, Trevor and Jan who picked up where the MMU 'gang' left off. Thanks also to Professor John Pratt, for his comments on an early draft of this book, and to Dr David Pearson for his advice. Special thanks go to Dr Liz Marr for invaluable support and advice on various chapters of this book.

There are many people who contributed to this book in numerous ways but special thanks also go to my parents Valerie and David Hutton for having faith in me and supporting me in my excursion into academia, which turned out to be a lot longer than I expected. An enormous 'thank you' goes to Steve who was always there and never wavered.

Introduction

Someone is writing about us – it's about time!

(Sophie research interviewee)[1]

As a one time avid clubber and participant in club spaces, the lack of literature available on women and their experiences of clubbing seemed puzzling at best and an unacceptable oversight at worst. The lack of space given to the discussion of female clubbers is all the more startling due to extensive press coverage of the death of Leah Betts,[2] and exaggerated tabloid reports of young women running amok in sexual frenzies under the influence of ecstasy (Williamson 1997; Collin 1997). Accounts of women's experiences have been told by men and appropriated into bizarre fantastical notions of how female clubbers behave when taking ecstasy and participating in club spaces. Did women not avidly and enthusiastically consume illegal drugs, alcohol and sex, style and music whilst negotiating night time streets and spaces? Had women not invested thoroughly in the 'new' culture of clubbing as consumers, DJs and promoters? Had they not marched in outrage at the proposed Criminal Justice Bill, which alas is now the Criminal Justice and Public Order Act 1994?[3]

Indeed they had done all of these things so *where were their stories*, their risks and pleasures, their highs and lows and what did it *mean* to be a female participant in contemporary club spaces in Manchester? Feminist research can tell us much about the social world through women's experiences (Stanley and Wise 1993), so my aim is to explore not only women's stories, but to challenge stereotypes of femininity and explore new discourses of and changing ways in which women express their femininity. Amongst the questions raised and discussed are the complex debates surrounding risk, pleasure, drug use and sex and whether these issues need to be explored in a new and different way. The research which underpins this book is important because it reveals what women's stories can tell us about societal attitudes towards risk, pleasure, femininity, sexuality, and whether these attitudes have changed – it is not *just* about storytelling.

---

1   Respondents names have been changed to ensure confidentiality.

2   Leah Betts was a young woman who died after taking ecstasy in 1995. Her parents gave permission for pictures of her in intensive care in hospital to be used in an anti-drugs campaign. Her death and the subsequent campaign were the subjects of intense scrutiny by the media.

3   The Criminal Justice and Public Order Act 1994 was a piece of UK legislation that banned outdoor gatherings or 'raves' and legislated against music with a certain number of beats per minute. Amongst other things it allowed Police to detain suspects for up to 28 days without charge and abolished the 'right to silence' upon arrest. There were widespread protests from all sections of society against what was considered to be a punitive piece of legislation.

My aim is not to chart in detail the progress of Manchester's club scenes, but to examine the phenomenon of clubbing from a gendered perspective to provide an analysis of participation in club spaces from the view of female clubbers. However the importance of Manchester in the development of club culture must not be underestimated. The continuing development of clubbing in Manchester is based on the enthusiastic consumption of style, music and drugs by 'youth'. Manchester in conjunction with other northern cities such as Sheffield marketed itself on its nightlife and as a hip culturally important place to live, work and play. The places of the now legendary Hacienda[4] nightclub and of equally legendary Manchester bands such as New Order, The Happy Mondays, and The Stone Roses, in this development have been recognized in many of the key accounts of 'rave' and dance culture (see Haslam 1999; Collin 1997). The rise of the Hacienda nightclub was central to the development of club cultures in Manchester, and the rise of the 'Madchester' image. This was also due to the antics and music of Manchester-based bands such as The Happy Mondays and The Stone Roses. In the 1980s the emergence of 'clubbing' provided a new focus for the study of youth. The combination of the drug ecstasy and new electronic forms of music facilitated an explosion in youth culture that is still prevalent today (Hunt and Evans 2003; Carrington and Wilson 2004). The 'rave' scene, as it was termed in the late 1980s and early 1990s, formed in – what is argued – very specific political and social circumstances; mainly those borne out of a disappointment with Thatcher's politics, but also linked to the Thatcher ethos of entrepreneurial spirit. This entrepreneurial spirit was evident behind the organization of the early illegal 'raves' in the late 1980s, and in part still exists within the booming cultural industries such as music production and fashion that have grown from the early seed of 'rave' culture. The development of club cultures in Manchester has also been charted as being linked to urban regeneration (Lovatt 1996). Manchester was promoted as a vibrant, cultured place and the idea of nightlife was incorporated into the marketing of Manchester as a city.

Before 1990 regulatory bodies such as the police were unenthusiastic about new, later licenses for pubs, clubs or bars, and the idea of the city at night was seen in terms of social dysfunction and problems such as violence. However as developments in 'rave' gathered momentum those involved in the cultural production offshoots demanded to be recognized by the regulatory bodies of the city council. The shift towards deregulation of the night time economy can be seen in the city council's encouragement of investment in urban redevelopment. Manchester was marketed as an attractive place for investment and the city's cultural and entertainments industries were expected to provide new jobs and to give Manchester a cosmopolitan image. The upsurge of clubs, bars and later licenses was also influenced by Manchester's Olympic bid of 1992–1993, and by the successful staging of the 2002 Commonwealth Games, which put the spotlight on the 'chic' of the city. So from unregulated, illegal

---

4   The Hacienda closed briefly in 1991 to protect staff from violence, reopening again three months later. It finally closed its doors in 1997.

'raves' grew new spaces for clubbing such as 'Home' and 'Sankey's Soap'.[5] The city of Manchester and its emphasis on night life and culture has become central to the development of clubbing. The right ingredients appeared to have come together just at the right time; entrepreneurs, music, new spaces for clubbing and a change in attitudes towards the city at night facilitated by extensive urban regeneration.

Methods on the Margins

This study has grown out of the need to explore the experiences of female clubbers. Having highlighted that these experiences are missing from previous discourses regarding club cultures, how can club scenes be investigated in ways that position the experiences of women at the forefront of the research process? One way to do this is to use ethnographic methods,[6] as it has been argued (Oakly 1985; Finch 1993) that ethnography is the best way to investigate the previously ignored position of women, such as female clubbers, in criminological research. Feminist standpoint methodologies therefore set out to make a key issue of the fact that women's voices can and should speak for themselves, so to give female clubbers a voice and to recognize their experiences as important, qualitative research methods were used. Clubbing as a leisure activity does not appeal solely to young people, i.e. those under 25. This is evident in the diversity of the female clubbers who took part in the research that underpins this book as they are a wide and varied group. The youngest was 21 and the oldest was 39, two identified as mixed race, four as working class, four were single parents, all were in some kind of employment although this varied from casual work such as bar staff or providing décor in clubs, to students, to teachers, to health care professionals, to self-employed businesswomen, to highly paid executives. Only one respondent identified herself as bisexual and one, although she had sexual experiences with same-sex partners, was not comfortable with this label. This particular sample of clubbers were mainly white, heterosexual, middle class and in their mid to late twenties and early thirties. Therefore in order to capture the experiences of such a diverse group of women flexible and dynamic methods such as ethnography are needed to change and keep pace with the research process.

In terms of methodology, criminology has ignored women because of its emphasis on positivistic facts-based research – the holy grail of criminology is after all to find the *cause* of crime, criminality and deviant behaviour. Therefore a feminist method

---

5 These two night clubs both had problems with violence and 'Home' closed in 1995, 'Sankey's Soap' closed in 1998, but reopened again in 2000.

6 Ethnography as noted by Fielding (1993) is a form of qualitative research that contains several methods including interviewing and observations. Qualitative interviews are regarded as one of the most widely used and useful research tools (Fielding and Thomas 1993) and are seen as most valuable as a research method to reach and research niche or marginalized groups. The data generated from qualitative interviews are valuable for their rich detail, and by using such a flexible method a dynamic research strategy develops which is important when studying social groups that are marginalized.

is needed in a research agenda that positions women such as female clubbers as having agency and being active in the construction of their identities. For feminist researchers the use of qualitative approaches such as in-depth interviews begins to give an understanding of women's lives and experiences. Thus for this qualitative approach to the study of club spaces and the experiences of young women in-depth, semi-structured interviews[7] were used as the main research tool. Female clubbers and recreational drug users are a marginalized group in society for several reasons. They break the law by consuming illegal substances, they are independent in terms of acting out femininities and sexualities and by virtue of their gender their experiences are not considered to be of enough value to research. Access to such marginalized groups is often difficult due to worries for the interviewees about confidentiality, especially about illegal activities such as drug dealing and drug use. However, as feminist writers have commented (Finch 1993) female research respondents are often pleased that somebody is asking for their opinion as this is rarely the case. The problem for researchers is not to misrepresent what is revealed and to deal sensitively with the information given.

Gender and Club Spaces

This book reflects the search for a revised agenda for rendering women and girls visible in contemporary forms of (sub)cultures such as club spaces. The invisibility of girls in early subcultural analyses is important as this set the agenda for a continuing struggle to get gender-based research recognized against a background of class as the definitive factor in sociological and criminological analysis. Through giving women a voice, this book addresses how and why they identify with each other and with clubbing as a lifestyle and a leisure activity. It explores how their identities are constructed through style, music, sexuality and drug use in the different arenas used for clubbing. The differences between club spaces and what they mean in terms of different formations of 'subcultural' style, social rules and behaviours are also discussed and analsyed.

One of my key theoretical foci throughout the book is that (sub)cultures are formed and developed in very different ways in a society that is fragmenting and changing. This therefore has implications for how issues such as drug use, sexuality and risk taking are explored and analysed. The way that young people and young women in particular take risks are often seen in a negative light. Risk taking in terms of young women, clubbing and drug taking can be explored in cultural criminological terms as fun, exciting and pleasurable (Ferrell and Sanders 1995). Although not all risk taking has a favourable 'safe' outcome, the pleasurable, exciting side to risk is important and is rarely addressed, especially in terms of the experiences of young women.

A further aim is to address the differing forms of social control that operate to constrain women within diverse clubbing spaces. Whilst more equal attitudes

---

7   In addition to in-depth interviews focus groups and participant observations were used to supplement the data from the interview material.

towards women are supposed to prevail, it is arguable whether this is substantiated by evidence of the participation of young women in such spaces. In fact the research that has explored youth cultures in terms of gender suggests that power relations and hierarchies still exist that are based on the gender of participants (see Thornton 1995). It is suggested that a level of control by men over women is considered as 'normal' and part of everyday life and this has been a useful tool for analysing how women experience such controls in the context of club spaces.

However, it is also significant that women involved in certain spaces of club scenes can feel empowered by their involvement. Constraints on women's expression of femininity and sexuality may also be seen in an analysis of 'new femininities' and of women's safety while negotiating the night time streets of city spaces. The significance of how spaces in the city are often contested by different groups and how this can lead to tension and conflict has been highlighted (Ryan and Fitzpatrick 1994), and an exploration of how these conflicts and tensions are expressed and resolved within different club spaces is presented here. In addition, this book addresses the issues surrounding young women and recreational drug use, and how this is interrelated with the expression and regulation of sexuality within club scenes in Manchester. The grounding of these concerns is discussed in more depth in the following chapters.

Chapter 1 introduces the themes and theoretical framework that this book was developed within. An analysis of ethnographic accounts of different club spaces and the development of the typology of *mainstreams* and *undergrounds* as a tool to explore difference and identities as constructs of *attitude* is presented in chapter 2. The importance of female producers of club scenes such as DJs, promoters and drug dealers, is highlighted in chapter 3, and the discussion focuses on how their gender affects the negotiation of these masculine worlds. This chapter is also significant as it explores the under-researched and under-theorized world of drug dealing from a female perspective.

The theme of risk and pleasure, whilst incorporating *attitude* in exploring the negotiation of drug use and sexual behaviour, is expanded in chapter 4. It is argued that women take part in risky behaviour, but derive pleasure from this behaviour in terms of challenging societal stereotypes in a 'safe' arena. Also discussed here is the extent to which club spaces are 'safe' for young women clubbers. For example do female clubbers feel that they can challenge stereotypes of femininity and sexuality within club spaces; can they experiment with drugs and sex, push the boundaries of femininity without being censored or punished for their behaviour/s? Or do young women feel constrained and pressured into having casual sexual encounters and acting out 'acceptable' femininities? The focus of discussion then moves onto risk and pleasure both in the context of travelling through the city at night and within the club scenes concerned. Chapter 5 also addresses sexuality and tolerance which are analysed in relation to the expression of different sexualities within different spaces. Safety and tolerance in club spaces are therefore linked to the *attitude* of others present. The final chapter then pulls the main themes of the book together and offers some concluding thoughts on the experiences of female clubbers.

Chapter 1

The Invisible Woman? The Participation of Women on Club Scenes

Introduction

Writing about subcultures in 2006 is an exciting, challenging and complex undertaking. The way that subcultural groups develop and reform is different in comparison to previous decades and even the notion of 'subculture' itself has been challenged. In researching and writing about the experiences of female clubbers a series of interconnected theories and debates are relevant. For example women who go clubbing move between and within spaces in terms of identity construction, although they tend towards identifying with a particular type of space, and the music and people within it. An observation that supports the notions contained within the post-subcultural debate that the term 'subculture' is no longer relevant in discussions of youth cultures. Alternatively female clubbers specify very clearly the types of spaces where certain groups of people belong and argue that club spaces are divided along 'tribal' lines. Here on the other hand the observations of female clubbers support the notion that the term 'subculture' is still relevant. Women who go clubbing highlight that difference and diversity are part of their experiences when participating on club scenes so it is important to recognize the differences between spaces that are termed the 'club scene', with implications for the different experiences of women within them. Tensions between traditional expectations of femininity and sexuality and the expression of these features of identity are also apparent for female clubbers which are in turn linked to the debates surrounding gender, risk and pleasure. These overlapping arguments serve to emphasize the complex nature of gendered debates and the fact that gender remains an interesting, fragmented and diverse category for academic research and discussion. Thus the arguments I will discuss further in this chapter present new questions about the nature of femininities, sexualities, risk and pleasure for drug-using women participating in club spaces at night.

It can be argued that the position of young women has changed within society, and that women are not as socially constrained as in previous decades. Therefore a more relevant research agenda based on exploring (sub)cultural groups in the public sphere, such as club scenes, is called for to look at the contemporary experiences of young women. This research agenda needs to focus upon the public participation of young women within (sub)cultural scenes, because their lives have changed. However, the male centredness of cultural studies is still apparent and in contemporary society this is now more problematic than ever (Pini 2001). Women and girls take part in cultures and spaces that render them visible in public and which also label them quite clearly as participants in these cultures and spaces. So why the reluctance of writers (Miles 2000; Calcutt 1998) to consider gendered experiences? In focusing on the experiences of female clubbers, the extent to which club spaces are actually empowering for women is a theme that also runs through this book. It is generally acknowledged that club spaces are more liberal in terms of attitudes toward women and that women suffer from less sexual harassment in these types of spaces. This is often associated with the use of the drug ecstasy. 'This resulted in some women finding dance events preferable to traditional straight night clubs because of the resulting reduction in sexual advances, propositions and harassment from heterosexual men' (Meesham et al. 2000, 38).

However as will be discussed in more detail in chapter 4, ecstasy-based club spaces are not necessarily the liberated spaces they are claimed to be, so how far do they really offer young women anything new in terms of empowerment and lack of sexism or harassment? Club scenes are sites of multiple struggles in terms of women asserting themselves within these spaces. Clubs are thought of as being 'safe' but the question of whether this is actually the case is explored throughout this book. The female clubbers were clear that overt harassing behaviour by men is not tolerated in some club spaces, but that this overt behaviour is replaced by more subtle covert forms of sexism. Women clubbers are involved in renegotiating spaces that are still dominated by male attitudes, so is sexual expression and availability the price they have to pay?

A further theme that is explored is that of difference and fragmentation. Commentators when writing about clubbing tend to categorize clubbing or club spaces as one scene or (sub)culture (Miles 2000). The material presented here highlights that this is clearly not the case with a diversity of clubbing arenas producing differing kinds of clubbing experiences particularly in relation to gender. In exploring difference however, the difficulty comes in the terms used for analysis. To define a complex group of social spaces such as clubs is always difficult but for the purposes of this discussion the terms underground and mainstream will be used to differentiate between the various kinds of spaces used for clubbing. The term underground itself is problematic as undergrounds define themselves in relation to authenticity of style and music (Thornton 1995). However the trickle up of underground styles and music into the mainstream is what is problematic for these types of club spaces – can we really state that true undergrounds do exist? The diversity of club scenes also suggests that more appropriate terms to differentiate between the spaces used for clubbing would be mainstream*s* and underground*s*.

Undergrounds with reference to the club spaces discussed here, refer to places that meet a number of criteria set out by female clubbers. Firstly the music played in these types of clubs is more experimental with DJs playing more cutting-edge music styles involving breakbeat[1] for example. Musical style is constantly changing and being

---

1   Breakbeat evolved from late 1980s rave and its attributes are 'funky rhythm tracks, lots of samples and choppy mixes, sped-up "chipmunk" vocal loops, frenetic explosive energy with

developed, but the important issue in underground spaces is the experimentation and the offering of 'something different' from mainstreams. Research has documented that different spaces attract different crowds and that this difference starts with the type of music played at a particular venue, which in turn influences drug use (Hunt and Evans 2003; Sanders 2005) and crowd demographics (Gore in Thomas 1997). Club cultures are fluid, unstable and fragmented and often defy definition. The differences in the spaces of undergrounds and mainstreams have implications for the experiences of women clubbers who attend in terms of safety, attitude and identity construction all of which will be explored further in later chapters.

Secondly the people attending have to have the right attitude towards others, especially women. Undergrounds were defined by female clubbers as places where less sexist and macho attitudes towards women were encountered. These better attitudes were associated with the types of drugs used, the lack of alcohol use, the music played and the style of those attending. *Attitude* is emphasized here as it is developed as a theoretical construct subtly related to style. *Attitude* is linked to where clubbing women choose to go and consists of a crucial range of factors that affect their night out, as a range of social and cultural factors that have to be present for women to feel 'right'. This feeling 'right' was associated with underground club spaces. *Attitude* is seen by female clubbers as underpinning everything else that is important about club spaces. Without the 'right' attitude clubbers both male and female are excluded from participating and for women within club spaces it is *attitude* that is the most important defining factor in determining who belonged where and feeling 'right'.

Thirdly, and this is linked to *attitude*, underground spaces are clubs that have an anything goes atmosphere towards fashion that is emphasized by the lack of dress codes.[2] This free atmosphere is also linked to feeling comfortable with same sex partners in terms of holding hands, hugging and kissing, so the lack of policing of behaviour by others in the space is also a feature of undergrounds. Undergrounds tend to be situated in smaller, less commercialized spaces that put on innovative nights with creative décor and new up-and-coming music styles. They tend to have an older age group, approximately twenty five and over, and are not as highly sexually charged.

Mainstreams refer to commercialized spaces for clubbing with musical styles that are often in the music charts, popularized and widely dispersed throughout youth cultures and wider society. *Mainstreams* can also refer to large clubs with a young age group, approximately sixteen to twenty two that are highly sexually charged spaces. The type of music played affects consumption of drugs such as amphetamines and

---

a speed of 135 to 170 beats per minute' (www.ethnotechno.com.defs.php). Breakbeat music is the sampling of breaks as drum loops (beats) and using them as a basis for hip hop tunes for example. More contemporary electronic artists and club DJs have created 'breakbeats' from other electronic music and fused them together. So this type of music is literally composed by 'breaking the beats' of other songs (http://en.wikipedia.org/wiki/breakbeat).

2   Mainstream club spaces have specific styles that have to be adhered to in order to gain entry such as no trainers, jeans or baseball caps.

the use of alcohol, producing a different *attitude* from the clubbers who use such spaces. Mainstream spaces as well as a younger age group attending also tend to have dress codes, and a less tolerant attitude towards those who are different. 'Rave' has been labelled as the last subculture (Miles 2000), because of the combination of alternative lifestyles and 'relentless production of commercialism' (Miles 2000, 98), although the commercialization and 'corporatization' of club spaces is something that female clubbers were very much against. In fact they moved from *mainstreams* to the *undergrounds* to avoid this commercialization of club spaces. *Mainstreams* were associated with high prices, chart based music, and poor sexist attitudes towards women (see chapter 2 for a more detailed discussion of these divisions).

So the divisions that are apparent within club cultures have an effect on the way in which young women engage in clubbing as a leisure activity and on the risks they take in these particular environments. Risk is looked at in a number of fields such as health, night club bouncers and governance (Dean 1999; Skidmore and Hayter 2000; Hobbs et al. 2003) but my focus will be on young women who go clubbing and I will analyse club spaces as new sites of risk and pleasure in terms of gendered experiences.

The Study of Club Cultures

Developments in clubbing in Manchester in terms of culture, music and violence[3] are discussed in masculine terms and focused on the experiences of young male clubbers (Collin 1997; Malbon 1998). In addition the discussion of subcultural style in the form of club cultures has a masculine tone or bias. For example Malbon (1998, 266) states that he wishes to look at the 'experience of clubbing' but again the focus is on young men who are taking part in this experience and female clubbers are absent from this discussion. While the experiences of young men within club spaces cannot be denied a place in the literature, the absence of accounts of clubbing from the perspective of female clubbers has left a large gap in the exploration and study of club cultures.

How identities are formed has been explored by researchers looking at club cultures (see Malbon 1998; Thornton 1995, 1997). Clubs are spaces in which clubbers identities are formed and reformed as they experience the event, and the contexts of social interactions are crucial in terms of the opportunities to identify with others. Identity and unification are seen as less significant in contemporary club spaces, and it has been argued that clubbers identify more with the actual space than those within it (Malbon 1998). Although space in the context of clubbing is certainly important, the question of identity and unification being less important has to be acknowledged as problematic. Identity and unification are not present in contemporary youth cultures in the same obvious ways as the 'punks' and 'mods' of the 1960s and 1970s, but are present in different more subtle ways. Identity and unification for female clubbers can be seen as crucial in terms of *attitude* and these

---

3   The demise of the focal points for clubbing and the upsurge in violence will be discussed in more detail in chapter 2.

differing types of identity formation are also fluid and can change quite dramatically; as Malbon (1998) points out there is movement *between* groups.

In analysing the spaces of clubbing, subcultural hierarchies exist that are based on subtle power relations that are at work within them where gender is significant. Youth cultures are stratified within themselves, and young people such as those who go clubbing seek out and accumulate cultural experiences for use within their own social worlds. These cultural pursuits involve a form of power brokering in which 'hipness' becomes a form of 'subcultural capital'[4] (Thornton 1995), that confers status on its owner. Club cultures contain hierarchies within themselves, which result not in a unified culture but fragmented clusters which share the term 'club culture', that maintain their own dance styles, music genres and behaviours. Club nights are culturally organized by an attitude which can be described as 'hipness'. Both gender and difference are therefore shown to be very much apparent within club spaces as are the power relations that work against young women in terms of their challenge to feminine stereotypes and the construction of alternative identities.

Subcultural groupings still reinforce stereotypical images of women as passive and uninvolved in the essence of these social spaces and groups. As parts of club cultures became perceived by participants as mainstream and 'unhip' they were feminized. Young women were objectified in unflattering stereotypes and placed outside the 'hip' places to be. The 'Sharon and Tracy' dancing round handbags[5] image of the unhip, unsophisticated clubber is embodied in such disparaging terms such as 'Techno Tracy's' (Thornton 1995, 100). This objectification of young women is a 'position statement made by youth of both genders about girls who are not 'one of the boys'. Subcultural capital would seem to be a currency which correlates with and legitimizes unequal statuses' (Thornton 1995, 104). Therefore women within club spaces are still looked upon in disparaging, dismissive terms and this is especially true when looking at the currency of 'subcultural capital' that women within club spaces are not seen to possess *because of their gender.*

This continuing negative, passive view of female clubbers results in the theoretical discussion of club cultures being focused on young males or of researchers assuming a masculine stance on what is researched. The moral panics generated by the police and media have centred on drug use and drug deaths, and young women if they

---

4   Thornton (1995) applies Bourdieu's theories of cultural capital to her own, developing the concept of 'subcultural capital'. Bourdieu's definition of capital is very wide. It includes material things, which can have a symbolic value, as well as culturally significant attributes such as prestige, status and authority. Cultural capital is defined as culturally valued taste and consumption patterns. For Bourdieu cultural capital can take different forms such as art or language, and capital acts as social relation within a system of exchange. Bourdieu also sees capital as a basis of domination, although this is not always recognized as such by the participants. Different types of capital can be exchanged for each other i.e. capital is 'convertible. The most powerful form of capital is symbolic capital, as it is in this form that various different types of capital are perceived and recognized as legitimate.

5   It must be noted that 'Handbag' itself became a particular form of music, albeit seen as less 'cool' or 'hip' than techno, garage or drum and bass.

are referred to at all are victims rather than perpetrators or active participants in club scenes (Redhead 1993). As the focus for discussion about this aspect of youth culture in popular representations has been elsewhere, it is important to explore the meanings that constructions of identities have for women participating in club spaces and whether their participation challenges a masculine patriarchal way of thinking and theorizing about young women who take drugs and dance in club spaces.

An apolitical view of club scenes is present in later accounts of clubbing which are critical of those who take part in these scenes for being apathetic politically and purely hedonistic (Calcutt 1998; Miles 2000). 'Rather they behave in ways that barely threaten the dominant order and which in many respects serve to bolster or re-energize that order' (Miles 2000, 89). However this type of stance explores (sub)cultures in Centre for Contemporary Cultural Studies (CCCS) terms which it is argued by some are now obsolete. In many ways this critique 'misses the boat' when investigating clubbing because gender and difference within club cultures are not considered. A hedonistic, non-challenging view of clubbers is presented, which is not the case when gender is taken into account. Although women are still treated in sexist ways in club spaces they very much challenge traditional concepts of femininity and sexuality and just being on club scenes as women is a challenge in itself that female clubbers revelled in. What is not recognized through inattention to gender is that clubbing has meaning for young women in terms of challenging who they are supposed to be.

In addition the assertion that the main incentive is to get 'blitzed out of your brain' (Miles 2000, 92) is not an adequate representation of female clubbers and why they take part in clubbing lifestyles. Of course part of the idea is to escape, to consume drugs, sometimes to excess, to lose yourself in the freedom of styles of music and dance that are closely integrated with drugs such as ecstasy, but the desire for oblivion? This has more resonance with injecting opiate users than it does with recreational drug users.

By underplaying the political significance of club cultures, Miles (2000) falls into the trap that Carrington and Wilson (2004) highlight, in that social inequality is under theorized. Clubbing is not about apathy, it is a rejection of a world that has failed clubbers and a move towards creating a new worldview – if only for the weekend. Although, *some* clubs offer women space to re-negotiate their femininity and sexuality and in ignoring gender and difference, both Calcutt (1998) and Miles (2000) ignore important aspects of club spaces and the politics that are involved at micro-level.

Postmodernism and Risk Theory

The fragmentation and diversity of club cultures has been linked by some writers (Muggleton 2000; Redhead 1993) to the theoretical framework of postmodernism. In simple terms the main issue for postmodern writers is that society is undergoing radical changes in how it is formed and that social life or social groups are therefore developed under very different circumstances. For example consumption rather than social class is seen as one of the most important features of identity construction for young people in contemporary society (Furlong et al. 1997). It is generally accepted that the subcultures of the 1970s are a phenomenon of the past with their reliance on social class and rebellion as central features of subcultural theory. However writers are divided on how important the 'old order' of macro concepts, such as class, are in contemporary society. It has been argued that social developments in terms of change and fragmentation have brought with them new freedoms, levels of consumption as well as new possibilities for individual choice (Giddens 1991). Postmodernism is also seen to have signalled the collapse of metanarratives (Lyotard 1984) with their privileged truth and that there is a move towards the plurality of voices from the margins being heard. So where does this leave researchers and writers looking at phenomena such as club cultures? How are these groups divided and what makes the members stick together?

One way of exploring changes in social groups is to argue that mass culture is breaking up, and that the remainders of mass consumption society are groups distinguished by their members' shared lifestyles and tastes (Maffesoli 1996). Female clubbers stated with some emphasis that groups of people can be identified within club scenes and attributed to a certain 'tribe' or 'tribes'. In discussing collectivities, a type of 'tribe', it is argued that they have certain powers of integration and exclusion and of group solidarity. Members of particular 'tribes' are seen as wearing certain types of clothes and adorning themselves in specific ways (Maffesoli 1996). The concept of 'emotional communities' (Maffesoli 1996, 12) that are found alongside the rigidity of institutions such as the workplace, and which are described by Weber as ill-defined and changeable, can be compared to club scenes which can be conceptualized as types of 'emotional communities'. They are not particularly organized, especially underground scenes but clubbing women felt that their participation was a release from the pressure of everyday life. Hence club scenes exist alongside the rigid social structures of everyday life such as the family and work. Women clubbers enjoyed socialising and using drugs for pleasure among people who thought in the same terms they did, or had a similar *attitude*. It is through these types of interactions that contemporary 'tribes' are formed 'Within the mass, one runs across, bumps into and brushes against others; interaction is established, crystallizations and groups form' (Maffesoli 1996, 73).

Another way of exploring changes in social life is through an analysis of risk, and in discussing risk Beck (1992) argues that the contemporary world is fundamentally divided by the distribution of risks in a society characterized by uncertainty and risk. In examining contemporary society, risk theorists (Beck 1992; Furlong et al. 1997; Giddens 1991) highlight that experimenting with drugs is a response made by young people to the 'risks' associated with living in a late modern society. The individual's relationship with risk and the uncertainty caused by postmodern society is one of control; how much control do people have over the risks that surround them, for example, young people's experience of the labour market, or poverty or racism. Young people are seen to react to the risks and inequalities in modern life by taking part in increasingly risky behaviour themselves, such as drug and alcohol consumption (Furlong et al. 1997). In terms of drug use the role of ecstasy has been seen as an antidote to the prevailing atmosphere of risk and uncertainty in modern society. Youth in contemporary society are seen as increasingly discontented and demotivated, and their use of ecstasy as a reaction to a society based on the negotiation of risks (Calcutt 1998). However this view of discontented and demotivated youth is not necessarily indicative of female clubbers and the reasons they take drugs and go clubbing. Ecstasy use can be a means of 'escape' for clubbing women but this is not necessarily negative and destructive escapism. Female clubbers, when using drugs such as ecstasy, escape from a number of things; work, family commitments, and stress *as well as* traditional concepts of femininity and identity. So, 'escaping' for female clubbers has a positive connotation and this also brings pleasure and excitement. Risk taking and the use of ecstasy are not necessarily seen in a negative light by female clubbers.

It is also important to be aware of the gender dimension of risk construction and management in contemporary society as the tendency in previous studies on women and risk taking behaviour has been to concentrate on women's risk avoidance behaviour, even if this is viewed in a critical way. What women can do to avoid risk is a common theme in academic and popular writing such as newspapers, women's magazines, and crime prevention literature (see Stanko, 1990, 1997). Women who take risks such as female clubbers are labelled as irresponsible and sexually deviant. Very little research has focused on women who take pleasure from their 'risky' behaviour. It is assumed that women will want to avoid risk, and risk is seen in very narrow, negative ways. 'What constitutes "risky behaviour" is filtered through a masculine lens that conditions what we define as risky. Moreover when women do take exceptional risks the tendency is to conflate women's exceptional risk taking with amorality as in the case of promiscuity' (Chan and Rigakos 2002, 743). Social theorists such as Beck (1992) tend to consider the gender dimension of risk primarily within the context of the private and domestic sphere, especially the family. The emphasis tends to be on specific gendered roles for women that can be viewed as conservative, therefore shifting the emphasis to public places such as clubs results in a different reading of the gendered nature of risk taking and risk management. Indeed female clubbers take great pleasure in 'risky' behaviour and revel in the excitement of taking part in the illicit night time economy so it is necessary to move away from only considering risk in a negative light.

In particular the individualization of risk situates it in a negative and problematic context as this throws into question the notion of social rights and is also linked to the way individuals govern themselves and others (Dean 1999). Thus as risk has become individualized 'we' are responsible for governing ourselves and those like us. Individuals are blamed for their failings or problems as they are not seen to be linked to macro issues such as gender. In terms of women and clubbing an avoidance of acknowledging the importance of these macro issues negates the importance of gendered experiences. Women who engage in risk-taking behaviour, such as female clubbers, are seen as being responsible for managing themselves and are consequently blamed when things go wrong. Risk is also seen as a means of maintaining cultural boundaries in contemporary societies. Hence particular groups are singled out as dangerous and 'risky', and others as a threat to society (Douglas 1966, 1969 in Lupton 1999). Those who deviate from the norm are identified as being at risk, and the implication of this is that risk is ultimately controllable as long as expert knowledge is utilized in its control. Therefore those who behave in a way that is unfeminine or non-conformist, such as women clubbers and drug users, are not only risky but pathological. They are in need of control or treatment so that their riskiness does not contaminate others in society, especially partners or children (Lupton 1999).

Women who participate in club spaces, as well as gaining pleasure in this participation, have to negotiate and assess risk in connection with choosing this clubbing lifestyle. Although risks do present themselves in club spaces, women learn to navigate or at least recognize these risks, and take action to counter them. While it cannot be argued that women clubbers come away unscathed, they learned to put in place safety valves to minimize risk and to enhance their safety. The pleasure women gain from participating in club spaces and being able to express their identities in a way that has meaning to them, balances the risks they take in doing so.

(Sub)cultural and Post-subcultural Theory

The concept of subculture and whether it is still useful to view groups of (mainly) young people in this way is a problem that has been grappled with by many recent researchers (Bennett 1999; Khan-Harris 2004; Muggleton 2000; Thornton 1995), and which is relevant to the discussion of gendered experiences of clubbing. The problematic nature of the term subculture is rooted in critiques of the Centre for Contemporary Cultural Studies (CCCS) 1970s research about youth subcultures. To condense a large amount of theoretical discussion into a basic idea, the problem with CCCS based research is now seen to be its rigidity, and its reliance on a narrow discourse for its analysis of youth subcultures. It is now argued that contemporary society, and with it the cultural 'comings and goings' of youth, have changed so much in the past 30–40 years that a re-evaluation and perhaps a rejection of the term subculture is urgently needed.

One of the main criticisms of CCCS research from the point of view of studying female clubbers is that it effectively ignored women and silenced the female voices of those women and girls who took part in (sub)cultural activities. As Pini (2001) highlights 'To state the problem crudely (for the sake of introduction) girls and women just do not attract the attention of youth cultural commentators' (Pini 2001, 4), something that quite alarmingly is still apparent in 2006. For this reason I am critical of the work of the CCCS, and in this book I return to the local, the community, the neo–tribe (Maffesoli 1996) to examine the meanings that participating in club cultures have for young women, and to conduct a discussion that includes an analysis of gendered experiences. Even though CCCS research has been criticized in terms of its attention to macro concepts such as social class, gender,[6] I argue, is a macro concept that cannot be ignored in analysing club cultures, particularly in relation to the empowerment (or not) of young women clubbers. To ignore gender in this instance as writers such as Malbon (1998) do, is to misrepresent the clubbing experiences of young women. The stratified nature of culture does still exist and structural inequalities have not disappeared, so for young women clubbers they are not rebelling against or challenging in CCCS terms, a dominant political regime, but a societal view of women, drug use, femininity and sexuality that they see as constraining and oppressive. Therefore structural conflicts such as those around gender are played out within club cultures in relation to sexuality and femininity and the risks that young women clubbers take in doing drugs and sex.

The development of a new way of thinking about (sub)cultures has been termed post-subcultural theory (Bennett 1999; Muggleton 2000), to address the less structured, more fluid groupings that occur in contemporary society. In this analysis of gendered clubbing experiences although style, drug use and the performance of sexualities are less constrained by rigid boundaries, there still exist defining features and associations that are highlighted for example, in the differences that are apparent on *mainstreams* and *undergrounds*. Group affinities have not completely disappeared and these still have significance for the experiences of female clubbers. If cultural identities and the boundaries between them are blurring and categories are becoming less meaningful, so social theory needs new ways of theorising these blurred indistinct groups, and the concept of *attitude* in clubs is meaningful here as it sets people apart, defines them and where they belong.

Thornton's (1995) work is important in reminding us that interactions on a micro level are part of the complex picture of club cultures. This can be clearly seen later on in this book in discussions about fragmentation and difference within club scenes themselves. Pini's (2001) work shows us that it is possible in some club spaces to challenge the old order of acceptable femininity and to create new ways of expressing feminine identity, although it is clear that sex, race and class bound identities do not disappear even if the lines between them are slightly blurred. However (re)negotiating feminine identities can be fraught with danger as well as pleasure as club spaces are not necessarily always filled with love and equality.

So it would seem that this book is attempting the impossible; to reject a meta-narrative of club culture/s to investigate the 'complexity of a forever moving and fragmented scene' (Carrington and Wilson 2004, 75), but to analyse this complex, forever moving and fragmented scene in terms of gendered experiences. In answer to the contention that 'post modernists do not appear to find inequalities of stratified youth cultures because they are not looking for them' (Carrington and Wilson 2004, 77), in the chapters that follow, inequalities and difference are very much apparent in terms of production in club spaces as well as participation by female clubbers.

---

6   As well as other macro concepts such as race, although it is beyond the scope of this book to analyse these concepts in addition to gender (See Carrington and Wilson 2004 in Bennett and Khan-Harris 2004).

Femininities: Challenges and Changes

The framework within which the construction of identities for women on club scenes is developed comprises a whole range of issues which have previously been excluded (Collin 1997; Malbon; 1998; Miles 2000), in relation to women. Style, music, drug use, language, and sexual behaviour are all issues important in the construction of women's identities on these scenes. The different spaces that make up club scenes are underpinned by differences in the *attitude*, style and musical taste of participants. So, for women the identity which matters within different club cultures is the identity they are constructing at the time in a particular space. What is termed the 'club scene' no longer exists as this 'scene' has become fragmented and it comprises different types of clubbing experiences attracting differing groups of people. Women are able to move *between* different clubbing experiences by shifting the focus of their identities accordingly, using style, drug use and *attitude* to 'fit in'. As McRobbie (1994) states 'girls – both black and white have been unhinged from their traditional gender opposition while the gender and class destiny of their male counterparts has remained more stable' (McRobbie 1994, 157–158). So it would seem that there is considerable confusion over what femininity is and how it should be enacted and performed, or that there are multiple sites of femininity in contemporary society – women and girls are not a homogenous category and will choose to perform a number of feminine roles.

In terms of femininities is there a case for empowerment and challenge when this is discussed in the context of contemporary spaces such as clubs? *Geographies of New Femininities* (Laurie et al. 1999) refers to the idea that young women are claiming spaces for themselves. The emergence in popular culture of icons of new femininity such as the 'Spice Girls' and 'Tank Girl', is leading cultural theorists to suggest that new types of femininity are emerging for young women which are 'both excessively and transgressively feminine' (McRobbie 1996, 36). Women within club spaces can be seen as an example of these new femininities as within club spaces female identities are linked to fluid and changing femininities and specifically to sexuality. Women in club spaces act out their new femininities according to where they are in order to 'fit in'. Thus it can be argued that any analysis of club scenes encompassing gender, must take as its starting point women's own view of their position in the different spaces of clubbing. The way in which individuals characterize and explain their own experience is of particular relevance when considering issues of gender identity. If women feel empowered in participating in club scenes, even if to outsiders their position looks subordinate, is this all that is important? The extent to which women feel empowered on club scenes, can be considered as *relative to anything else they have encountered so far.*

This raises the question of whether in asserting their own choices and decisions – in what is still a male dominated sphere of popular culture – these spaces can be sites of feminine resistance to gender power. It can be speculated whether in contemporary club spaces an open attitude to gender equality really exists, or whether the supposedly 'free' atmosphere masks more complex power relationships that still act to subordinate women. An aspect of these issues of empowerment or subordination is that of how far women have created their own spaces to define their femininities.

An important part of the female voice is silenced in discussions about femininity as feminist theories are criticized for not looking at girls' *relations between themselves*. Relations *between* women on club scenes are of utmost importance with women supporting each other in terms of drug use and sexual safety. How women support each other in these ways, and how women treat each other, are part of the code of social rules that relates to *attitude*. Others both within and outside the club scene may censure women taking part for 'inappropriate' behaviour, but the female clubbers themselves do not.

Female identity and femininity have been present in previous subcultural groupings such as punk. In revisiting the subcultural scenes of earlier decades, identity negotiation in the specific social and public spaces of Punk have been re-examined (Miles 1997). Women's experiences of femininity within punk subcultures was positive in that they were able to express their identities and differing ideas of femininity freely in this context, although the negative aspect to these experiences is that within punk subcultures women were not seen as equals by the men involved. This was highlighted in activities such as 'slamming' on the dance floor when women are expected to leave the dance floor or accept the violent consequences (Miles 1997). Subcultures and club cultures therefore do not escape societal definitions of femininity and female places in youth cultures are not fixed because they are constantly transforming and modifying themselves. What is needed is an analysis which concentrates on localized politics of resistance, empowerment and experience that would consider for example, how women see their own femininities and sexualities and how these are related to their chosen form of representation.

Female clubbers do not lose their identities, they consolidate them when out clubbing (Pini 2001), and for clubbing women their pleasure is in consolidating identities that challenge traditional stereotypes of what they should be. This is what is significant about clubbing for a majority of women as they can explore and slip into alternative identities within the spaces of club cultures, even if it is only for the weekend. But with the focus of much research being on teenage girls, adult femininities are a much under-researched area (Pini 2001). Adult femininities such as those developed by female clubbers are often different compared to the traditional roles of wife and mother, which seem to be somewhat redundant when referring to clubbing women.

In trying to break out of particular stereotypes within the framework of a masculine hegemonic culture, female clubbers challenge some feminist writers who argue that girls do the work of that culture by positioning themselves and others inside acceptable guidelines of behaviour (Hey 1997). While this may be true to some extent what is important when examining club spaces are the relations between women on these scenes, and how far their experiences take them beyond these acceptable guidelines. Girls used the sense of the 'other' or 'othering' to distance themselves from undesired social relations and this use of the 'other' is also true of women within some parts of club scenes. However in this instance the 'other' is subverted and seen as representing *conventional* forms of femininity and this is what clubbing women want to distance themselves from, not vice versa.

Contemporary discussions of femininity have provided the division of girls into 'at risk' or 'can do' which produces images of girlhood that embody either success or failure (Harris 2004). However this discussion addresses what can be termed the shades of grey, as teenagers get older and grow into womanhood. What happens to the 'at risk' or 'can do' girls when they reach their twenties and thirties and how can clubbing women be categorized within this typology; are they more 'can do' than 'at risk' or vice versa? Girls have always been regulated and found themselves under scrutiny based on their sexual reputations (Lees 1997), but the way girls are regulated and categorized in late modernity has changed. Young women are increasingly seen as society's moral future with moral panics about their behaviour which could partly explain why there is such intense panic about female drug users and clubbers. It could equally explain why young women are so happy to find places and spaces where they can escape the regulation of their lives to some extent. This dividing of successful and failing girls is related to individualized success or failing which is criticized by risk theorists (Beck 1992). They argue that risks are unevenly distributed in society, and although risk is related to structural inequalities such as poverty individuals are blamed for their failure to succeed. It would seem that acceptable femininity for the 'can do' girl is based on effort by the individual which will produce success. Harris (2004) highlights that the way the media has embraced success, for 'can do' girls is detrimental not only to them but also to those who cannot or do not want to obtain those dizzy heights of 'beauty *and* brains, love *and* money, glamour *and* power' (Harris 2004, 19). It is a version of the 'superwomen' idea that was criticized by feminists that women had to have children and a career and look good too, being just a mother or just having a career was not enough. Femininity it is argued is also integrated with success in employment and those girls who do not 'make it' are viewed with suspicion and the idea that they have simply not tried hard enough to succeed and not put in enough effort. Inherent in this view of femininity is the idea that gender is denied, it is irrelevant and definitely not a hindrance. The notion of being a girl is associated with power as well as success and discrimination is something that is obscured. This however neatly sidesteps the issue of structural gendered inequalities and the fact that they are still very much apparent in contemporary societies. What about the other side of the coin, the 'at risk' girls who are very much constrained by structural inequalities such as gender and class? It would seem that 'can do' girls only 'do' when they come from wealthy and privileged backgrounds. Club spaces do not escape the structural inequalities regarding the construction of femininity, so whilst young women may be able to escape the rigours of gendered divisions these do not disappear completely. 'At risk' young women are those who are deemed to have failed and those who are also thought to be the risk takers but how does this apply to female clubbers? While it is always problematic to divide complex groups into categories it would seem that there are shades of grey that are not addressed here. Can a young woman be a risk taker and also a success? Are young women who go clubbing and take drugs (risk takers) failures or 'can dos'? Some of the young women presented in this book belonged to both groups; they were successful young professionals who were clubbers and drug users, so while their public work face was 'respectable' their public night time face was problematic.

Challenging Stereotypes? Sexuality and Club Spaces

Any discussion about nightlife and drug taking needs to take into account issues regarding sexuality and sexual behaviour and in terms of these issues club spaces are generally argued to be places where women can take part in drug taking, dance and abandonment without fear of harassment and sexist behaviour from the men that are present. Although Meesham et al. (2000) also caution against being too over zealous in stating that sexual interaction is lacking

> There is a danger of overstating the case here, however. Young people attending dance clubs in the 1990s were not asexual, automaton dance machines. If dance clubs were high on sexual or sensuous feelings but low on sexual activities, there was still the prospect of sexual activity occurring in the 'come down' period, at least for some.
>
> (Meesham et al. 2000, 40)

Therefore clubs are not necessarily places where there is an avoidance of sexuality and sexual behaviour and I will examine whether constructions of female sexuality are less constrained by stereotypical images of how women should behave. Club spaces are often thought to be liberating places with an 'anything goes' atmosphere but are they really? The experiences of female clubbers would suggest that young women who go clubbing face pressure to be sexually expressive and have casual sex. Therefore contemporary club spaces still involve women clubbers negotiating the pleasurable experiences of their sexuality within the constraints that 'openness' about sexuality leads to. For young men and young women who operate under the 'male in the head', there was no room, no language for a 'female in the head'. Research into young women and sexuality focuses on teenage adolescent experiences and it has been highlighted that young women construct their sexuality according to the 'male in the head' – the power of male dominated heterosexuality and of primary concern was the absence of female desire and pleasure in young women's accounts of their sexuality (Holland et al. 1996). Women it is argued are under pressure as adolescent girls to lose their sexual voice as they move into adult femininity. Girls who struggle to keep their full sexual voice are seen as causing trouble. Conceptualising female power is uncomfortable for both young men and women as it disturbs the available categories relating to how sexualities are thought about (Holland et al. 1992). This highlights that women who are in their twenties and thirties are an overlooked group for research even by feminist academics, in terms of sexuality, femininity and drug use. As Pini (2001) states 'Such women have most usually been studied in relation to "in home" activities such as television viewing and romance reading' (Pini 2001, 3).

This also focuses on one of the central problems for feminism – how can a positive female sexuality be conceived when there are only negative conceptions of the desiring female? The construction of femininity and sexuality as constraining for young girls and 'the importance placed on their sexual reputation acts as a constraint on female independence and desire' (Lees 1997, 4) again emphasizing that young women simply cannot express their sexualities in an adequate way as there is no language for this – there is no 'female in the head'. Whilst most studies surrounding sexuality have focused on young teenagers and adolescent girls there is little research on and interest in older women such as the clubbers discussed here. So while it may be true that adolescent girls are constrained by a narrow 'male in the head', how have young women in their twenties and thirties moved on from this 'male in the head' and do they have a more positive view or a better understanding of their own sexuality, have they found a 'female in the head' that was so impossible to express in their teenage years? The female clubbers discussed have made some progress in constructing alternative sexual identities and are moving towards a 'female in the head'.

However, women in negotiating their identity within subcultures have to renegotiate dominant discourses and ideologies of femininities. In this sense subcultural spaces also provide a form of resistance as the subcultural space of punk for example, did not escape society and its inequalities based on gender, but it provided a forum in which some women were able to renegotiate traditional feminine identities (Miles 1997). While women are able to explore their own identity within punk, relations between men and women were far from equal. This suggests that whilst alternative identities may be constructed outside the constraints of the 'real' world of work and family, this does not mean that women in subcultural spaces will necessarily be liberated from the constraints of female sexuality, constructed in that particular space or spaces.

However as research (See Holland et al. 1992, 1996, 1999; Hey 1993; Lees 1993, 1997) concentrates on young adolescent girls when examining issues relating to sexuality, one of my aims is to explore whether these observations still impact on older clubbing women who are in their twenties and thirties. Are their experiences in club spaces still shaped by their adolescent experiences of constraint and oppression, or is it a major attraction that club spaces hold for female clubbers that these spaces are not governed by the same rules, not even *mainstreams*? But is the behaviour of women in club spaces still defined by their sexuality and if so how much are they in control of this? As Lees (1997) argues 'all kinds of social behaviour by girls have a potent sexual significance' (Lees 1997, 21), so it is not *just* about sexual acts, women's behaviour of all kinds is monitored and this is just as relevant to clubbing women as to 'normal' women. There are some issues relating to risk, drug use and sexuality that hold true for women everywhere in the night time economy not just on club scenes.

Risky and Dangerous? Drugs and Drug Using Women

The exclusion of women in debates around substance use can be seen in discussions of subcultural groups such as mods and hippies. Women in such subcultures have been involved in drug use but they have not been given the attention of their male counterparts. The mod culture that grew up in the 1960s had much more appeal for girls, who were just as scrupulous in their style as their male counterparts (McRobbie and Garber 1975). The use of 'purple hearts' and other amphetamines were central to mod culture and although accounts of Mods do not explicitly refer to women's use of these drugs (Barnes 1991), it would be implausible to imagine that women who attended mod clubs did not use the same drugs as the men who were involved.

Similarly the Hippie cultures that developed used particular drugs that were suited to the Hippie ethos, and the music linked to that scene, such as acid and cannabis. The Hippie movement or counterculture, particularly in America, considered itself to be anti-establishment and the drugs used served to emphasize the differences between Hippies and 'them' (the establishment) (Miller 1991). Acid especially was seen to be a drug that expanded the consciousness that took the user to new levels of enlightenment. This was linked to the feeling within the Hippie movement that a social revolution was needed as Americans were 'culturally confined' (Miller 1991, 29), and that new ways of organising society as a whole needed to be found. The Hippie movement also included women, and although there is no explicit reference to women using drugs, as with the Mod culture, it would be naïve to assume that women did not indulge in the use of acid and cannabis. However the focus on the Hippie girl was on her sexuality, and the fact that she was seen as immoral. Therefore even in the case of the largely middle class 'hippy' subculture, women's participation reflected the 'double standard' inherent in society. Media moral panics only made women visible when their sexuality was seen as a threat, as in the 'hippy' cultures that were seen as sexually permissive. This is related to the historical discussion of women and drugs through the ages; that women who use drugs are also often seen as being sexually deviant or 'tragic'. This deviant behaviour is often seen as being specifically linked to music, location and time, as can women's use of ecstasy within club spaces. The suggestion therefore is not that the 'deviant' behaviour associated with drug use and sexuality for women is new, but that the emphasis is on locating women's experiences as important within the context of club spaces is.

In popular representations women who use drugs are often seen as bad or mad, risky, dangerous or tragic and any notions of pleasure, excitement and fun are not touched upon. These attitudes can be looked at historically, forming the basis for discussion of drug-using women; stereotypes from the 1920s still influence how women drug users in contemporary society are seen (Khon 1992). The idea of control, contamination and ruin of women comes out strongly in representations of women's drug use in the 1920s from the debates of the period centring on opium and cocaine use among women. This is an historically contingent view of young women as a social group with their own norms and values, although women drug users at this time were seen as 'victims', not as making their own choices or determining their own fate (Khon 1992). Drug use was an affront to femininity and society's view of what women should be and excuses were therefore made about the types of women that were commonly thought to be at risk of developing addictions; those with diagnosed 'nervous disposition', in other words unstable or 'risky' women. It was entirely unacceptable to suggest that women could choose to use drugs in a recreational manner and 'Whether they played the part of victim or harpy, the women of the drug underworld were of an uncontainable class' (Khon 1992, 5).

These women were a challenge to stereotypical images of femininity, and to the controls exercised over women in a patriarchal society. For women it is not the physical or psychological way that drugs may affect them, but the reaction to the fact that they are using drugs at all (Khon 1992). A critical view of the pleasurable aspects of women's drug use, that this risks 'feeding the negative stereotype of the selfishly pleasure-seeking female drug user' is still present in contemporary work (Meesham et al. 2000, 45). However what is wrong with women selfishly seeking pleasure through the use of drugs – nobody worries that young men will selfishly use drugs for pleasure. What is wrong with the pursuit of pleasure? Perhaps this critique of pleasure seeking is born out of the desire for women to be taken seriously and not portrayed as superficial, and that to be pleasure seeking is not political or significant enough in trying to develop an alternative reading of women's experiences. But for women who so often deny themselves at the expense of others surely being out and indulging themselves is both empowering and political from a personal perspective?

In considering these issues of pleasure and drug use it must be noted that the relevance of drug use occurring in a subcultural context has been questioned and it is argued that drug use has been normalized within society. However research clearly shows that whilst drug use is considered the norm in clubbing groups this cannot be generalized out into wider society, and given the assertion that non drug using clubbers are a significant group (Hunt 2003 and Evans, 5), care needs to be taken about oversimplifying this issue. It is true that some young people who are recreational drug users themselves have this view, that drug use is normalized, but it cannot be concluded that those outside this group feel the same. Also some female clubbers would argue that the way some other groups who participate in club spaces use recreational drugs in a club setting is deviant and destructive.

The distinction must also be made clear between recreational use of drugs, as with women clubbers, and dependent use of drugs such as heroin. Prostitution often accompanies addiction in women (Rosenbaum 1985) and this type of behaviour due to addiction is not usually present with women who use ecstasy. Recreational drug use within club scenes in this context is unusual as on the one hand it would appear that women can be visible and pleasure seeking in their leisure pursuits. But on the other, as will be explored further in chapters 4 and 5, there are still constraints on women within these scenes to conform to stylized sexual images of what women should be.

The problem of explaining issues surrounding young women and use of drugs such as ecstasy is just that; they are seen as a problem. Previous models of drug taking that focus on opiate use are not relevant to discussions about recreational use of drugs such as ecstasy. One of the first accounts which uses the term 'recreational drug use' is found in Henderson (1996), who is critical of the opiate-injecting model of drug taking which focuses on people excluded from the world of work and defines them as being passive victims of the drugs they use, and of those who supply them. This model is not relevant to the recreational drug use which is found in club spaces so recreational drug use needs a model which focuses on people engaged in consumption, with drugs such as ecstasy being consumed in public and rooted in mainstream culture, as opposed to the private marginalized use of opiate-based drugs (Henderson 1996). Drug use when looked at in this different way, instead of being seen as a problem can be seen in the light of fun, pleasure and excitement. Femininity in the context of injecting opiate use is seen as passive, dependent and deviant going against 'normal' female behaviour. On the other hand femininity in a clubbing context involves a more fragmented set of identities with the potential for 'More equal difference between the sexes' (Henderson 1996, 37).

In exploring the issues related to drug use there is also the stereotype of the 'self styled bad girls' (Harris 2004, 29). The suggestion is that use of drugs such as ecstasy produce this image of femininity and girlhood, but is this necessarily the case? Female clubbers would challenge this assumption although they were mainly middle class, and in some ways therefore protected by this class status. Women who choose to use drugs such as ecstasy are not necessarily looking to be bad girls – they may challenge stereotypes of femininity and sexuality and be independent but they are not necessarily highly criminal or 'bad' in a criminological sense. Also 'such young women are frequently represented and treated as risk takers who are increasingly disinhibited in their actions and must be monitored not simply for self destructive behaviour, but for potential harm to others' (Harris 2004, 29). Thus young women who indulge in casual sex, chaotic drinking and drug taking are monitored which is related to the regulation and control of young women – is clubbing and recreational drug use a way of escaping this societal gaze which tells women that to have fun is 'bad'? Tis touches on one of the focal points of this book, that to have sex, drink and take drugs is 'bad' and any notion that this type of behaviour can be fun, exciting and pleasurable seems to have been sidelined by researchers. Girls and young women may be labelled as 'bad' when they are simply having fun and enjoying themselves and it must also be noted that not all drug use, drinking and sex leads to the 'dire' consequences of single parenthood, poverty and problematic drug use.

Club Scenes, Leisure and Public Spaces for Women

In exploring how women can renegotiate traditional ideologies of femininity within club spaces, it is also important to consider gender issues in the use of the city as a site of leisure. Whilst young women today can access the city for leisure there are still constraints on those who do so which can be explored in terms of Victorian, patriarchal attitudes which shaped urban development. Despite the changes th.. have taken place in women's lives, and in the everyday life of the city, there are still ideological constraints originating from that Victorian period that continue to have resonance for female clubbers today.

In rapidly developing urban areas, women were seen as 'disorderly' and in need of control because disease, immorality and contamination were associated with them. Women's presence in the city was seen as a problem because it symbolized the promise of sexual desire which was converted into a moral and political threat (Wilson 1991). The city could be a place of liberation for women, which offered them the freedom to indulge in the pleasures and excitement it had to offer, but it could also be a place of danger for women, as witnessed in the dominant discourse of prostitution in urban life. For a woman to be in the city alone was to invite censure as a 'public' woman (a prostitute) (Wilson 1991).

To some extent even in the modern contemporary city this nineteenth century legacy of the 'public' woman being a 'fallen' woman still prevails. Traversing the city at night is still problematic for women, as streets and public spaces are still defined as male space. In the nineteenth century women became a target for surveillance and control, especially women who did not meet the acceptable images of respectable feminine behaviour in relation to sexuality. Women whose appearance, behaviour or associations contravened the definition of women as passive and restrained forfeited their claims to respectability and protection (see Khon 1992, Wilson 1991). In contemporary society women also face constraints on their use of the city as a site of leisure and these constraints are still very much based on respectability and the performance of acceptable forms of femininity. Heterosexuality is part of a whole package of behaviours that are defined by the values of a patriarchal society. It is seen in terms of manner and appearance, not just sexual orientation. If women do not conform to this 'package', they are punished for their transgressions by the threat of violence. Things have changed for women in contemporary society as it is now acceptable for women to be in public, but if they are to be 'public women' then they must still face consequences related to how they 'behave'. For women on club scenes there is an absence of this type of control and club spaces are viewed in general as 'safe' spaces, although it is travelling to and from these designated 'safe' spaces that is problematic for female clubbers using the city at night.

Young women clubbers who utilize city spaces at night are seen as disorderly in their consumption of alcohol, drugs and sex just like their Victorian counterparts (Griffin 1997 cited in Harris 2004, 28). Therefore 'girl power' utilized in a middle class 'good' setting is acceptable, but utilized in the spaces of the street it is unacceptable, so girls and young women are regulated to the extent that they are even told where they can be 'empowered'. Some sections of the population are also seen as abusing their 'girl power' rights to be assertive independent and confident. Female clubbers suffer from a backlash of this type of thinking and whilst it may be argued that in club spaces young women can find a place where they can be themselves, feel empowered and unconstrained by conventional controls on their sexuality, negotiation of outside spaces teaches them that they cannot step too far

daries. Even within club spaces forms of sexual violence and threat
ar on women who utilize girl power in an 'unacceptable' way.
erience and management of danger, and their personal safety outside
ere is the focus for much research but while criminologists have
nt crimes committed by strangers, women's lives are marked by a
continuum of male violence. Negotiating danger is in many ways negotiating power,
and women have more to fear from private than public violence (Stanko 1990, 1997).
Women are also used to taking responsibility for their own safety so this means they
have to juggle safety precautions with independence and autonomy. Women want to
live and lead normal lives, but put themselves 'at risk' in the eyes of society if they
do so. Women clubbers are no different in this respect and are conscious of their
personal safety, especially when leaving clubs at the end of a night out and although
private violence is the type of violence that women are most vulnerable to, the fear
of violence or assault restricts women's access to public spaces of leisure activities.

Even if these fears are not necessarily grounded in truth women's perceptions
about their safety will affect their behaviour. Sexuality is a crucial element when
looking at representations of how women and men spend their leisure time (Green et
al. 1990) and this is particularly apparent when looking at women and access to pubs
and their development as a form of leisure space. Historical studies of pub culture
show that pubs that developed from Victorian times are a male preserve. Women
alcoholics were looked upon as 'mad' or 'bad', and alcoholism or drunkenness was
associated with promiscuity (Hey 1986), in the same way that female drug users are
labelled. Club spaces do not have this recreation of patriarchal beliefs and values,
although this does depend on the type of club spaces used, with some spaces being
seen as safer than others. In general *mainstreams* were thought of as 'unsafe' for a
number of reasons related to drug and alcohol use and *attitude. Undergrounds* where
drug and alcohol use were different in comparison were seen as 'safe'. *Attitude*
is significant here as high alcohol consumption for example was seen to produce
the kinds of attitudes towards the control of women's sexualities that have been
oppressive to women in their use of the spaces and places of the city at night. 'Thus
a notable distinction for dance clubs was their relative physical safety for women,
and also for men too, without the threat of alcohol-related aggression' (Meesham et
al. 2000, 39).

A majority of women feel uncomfortable without a male escort in pubs and clubs
and as a consequence of being alone, unwanted male attention is not uncommon.
Spaces that are part of club scenes differ from this in the expected 'norm' for male
behaviour. Men are expected to have the 'right' attitude towards women and not take
part in overtly sexist behaviour. Women's access to leisure is not restricted in club
spaces as it is in pubs as clubbing women are very visible and thoroughly engrossed
in their experiences. Consumerism permeates the places and spaces of club based
leisure and consumption within the city is significant in terms of negotiation of
identities and a sense of belonging. This generates meanings of space and place, and
the ways in which the individual makes sense of the city, and reads its spaces and
places, are products of this negotiation of identities.

The following chapters give female clubbers a voice in a debate that has excluded them for the reasons referred to throughout this chapter. The tensions and conflicts experienced by female clubbers are explored and how they express and resolve these tensions and conflicts within different club spaces is the focus of my analysis. How do women who go clubbing take risks and balance these risks with pleasure and fun whilst keeping themselves safe? How do female clubbers perform femininities and sexualities in ways that challenge traditional ideas of who they 'should' be, negotiate safety in the spaces of the city at night, and how do they experience the use of drugs such as ecstasy interrelated with the expression and regulation of sexualities and femininities within club spaces? These questions are posed and explored throughout an analysis of what it means to be a female participant in the night time worlds of club spaces.

The grounding of these concerns and questions about female clubbers and their experiences will be discussed in further depth in subsequent chapters, beginning with an exploration of difference and diversity through style and music choice. Female clubbers' negotiation of the diverse club spaces that are on offer and how their gender affects their consumption of these spaces is examined in chapter 2.

Chapter 2

Gendered Experience of Club Spaces

Introduction

By choosing a clubbing lifestyle, women can renegotiate aspects of everyday life in ways that have meaning for them in terms of their sense of identity and their performance of gender and sexuality. For example, being in a 'wrong' place in terms of dress codes, means women's sexuality can suddenly become visible in terms of the *attitudes* of others within club spaces. The identities and meanings that female clubbers construct within club spaces, challenges the view that they are passive and uninvolved in these spaces. This aim of this chapter is to codify the differences between mainstream and underground club spaces, and to use these divisions as a theoretical tool in investigating style, taste, choice and sexualities. 'Difference' relating to *mainstreams* and *undergrounds* will be explored and how this affects the choice of spaces by female clubbers is illustrated by the data presented. Also discussed here is the significance for women clubbers of the range of club spaces to be found in Manchester, whilst developing further the typology of *mainstreams* and *undergrounds* introduced in chapter 1. Club scenes can be described as diverse spaces with different clubs playing different types of music, catering for different people. Therefore the mix of club nights on offer create a diversity of atmospheres which attract a wide range of people, with a variety of participants attracted to different sorts of 'scenes'. The differences between *mainstreams* and *undergrounds* are first explored in this chapter by outlining two 'typical' club nights,[1] described in terms of atmosphere, the types of people who attend and how this affects the experiences of female clubbers. This is followed by an analysis of how different participants on these scenes describe and account for their experiences.

An Underground Club Night

The first account is of what could be termed an underground club night. It is quite small scale, attracting a mix of people, but mainly an older age group (approximately twenty five to forty years) who have been attending since it started, about ten years ago. This type of club night is typical of *undergrounds* in Manchester. It is held in a small intimate venue, with most clubbers who attend knowing others from being on this scene for a number of years.

---

1 The data in this section was obtained by participant observation in the club spaces described. The descriptions of these spaces are supplemented by information and quotes from interviews conducted.

Going in the door there are friendly staff who smile and say 'hello'. The amount to get in is reasonable; five or six pounds. If you are on the guest list (which means you do not have to pay to get in), you are waved through, or you pay a reduced price. The door staff are very laid back with a tendency to let off familiar faces if they do not have enough money.

Once past the door you walk through a small room with the cloakroom, toilets, and a small space draped off where people can go to 'chill out',[2] chat or sit down if they need to. Through into the main room there are some tables and chairs arranged at one end with a 'herbal highs' stall (legal herbal alternatives to ecstasy, acid, and amphetamines). The bar is on the left side opposite. From here you can see down to the far end of the room where the DJs are and you can hear the music. Drapes and decor section off this area giving the impression of cosiness, and breaking up what is a large, long room.

The crowd who attend are very mixed, people of all ages, races and social groups. The drug emphasis is on ecstasy and cannabis and the atmosphere is friendly and relaxed. However the use of drugs in clubs has changed with less ecstasy and more cocaine and alcohol being used. This is due to the quality of ecstasy available being poor, so some clubbers turned to other drugs, and perhaps some had burned themselves out taking too much ecstasy. Therefore the atmosphere even in this club night, although relaxed and friendly, can sometimes be a bit fraught with groups of men being aggressive on the dance floor. The aggression is not overt. The young men concerned tend to push their way through the dance floor when it would make sense to go round, as it is busy. They dance too closely to other people and give the impression, through hostile stares for example, that they would be 'up for a fight'. Others on the dance floor just ignore them or move away as nobody wants a confrontation and, if ignored, they tend to drift away, as they have not got the reaction they wanted. Incidents like this make people feel less safe to take drugs and really let their hair down. This, coupled with the intimidating behaviour of a group of young men who usually stand near the DJ box, staring at people, and brushing past too closely when they move from 'their' spot, can make the atmosphere feel tense.

However in this space clubbers usually tend to drift around meeting up with friends in the bar area, have a drink, and, after socialising for a while, take some ecstasy and head for the dance floor. The music varies, but is usually breakbeat or 'dub'[3] based with a bit of techno[4] thrown in for good measure. People dancing are

---

2   The problem of clubbers getting too hot and dehydrating on the dance floor is recognized by some clubs who make a big effort to provide cooler, calm spaces for clubbers who need to rest and 'chill out' from the fast pace of their night out.

3   Dub music is a sub-genre of reggae music. In the 1990s and beyond dub has been influenced by and in turn influenced techno, jungle, drum and bass house music trip hop ambient music, and hip hop with many tracks produced by nontraditional musicians from these other genres. (http://en.wikipedia.org/wiki/Dub_music)

4   Techno is a form of electronic music that emerged in the mid-1980s and primarily refers to a particular style founded in America with influences from Germany and developed in and around Detroit and subsequently adopted by European producers. The term "techno"

usually stoned or 'luved up' under the effect of ecstasy, so the friendly atmosphere extends to the dance floor. If someone falls over, they get picked up, hugged, dusted off, and if people bump into each other, apologies follow. There is a communal atmosphere with the trading of drinks, such as water, and 'spliffs' with strangers.

The dress code is very laid back and those who attend wear anything from PVC to jogging bottoms. The very fashionable, glamorous, i.e. designer dresses and strappy high heels, club wear is not really apparent, and some people who are this dressed up look a bit uncomfortable. Most people wear casual comfortable clothes with a fair sprinkling of designer labels.

Dealers are out and fairly obvious. There have been problems in the past with people getting ejected for dealing, so although the club tolerates it, it pays not to be too obvious. All in all, clubbing in this space creates a friendly relaxed night, with a mix of people who are tolerant of each other. Those who attend know they will be looked after if anything goes wrong. They also tend to have a lot of experience of taking a variety of drugs in a club environment and can look after others if they are having a difficult time. Ambiguous sexualities such as women hugging and kissing or holding hands, who could be lovers or friends, are not challenged and there is a general atmosphere of 'anything goes', although this can depend on who is there. Some female clubbers mentioned specific men who were aggressive towards any same sex affection. They felt that how comfortable the night was, depended on the mix of people attending and how open their attitudes were. Some of the more aggressive men might try intimidating behaviour such as staring or following people round the club, but it usually goes no further.

The women's toilets are an interesting space within this club. The women in the inevitable queue tend to look after one another, which may be due to the mix of ages and people in general. On one occasion I observed a young woman who had taken too many drugs being ushered to the front of the queue because she felt sick. Afterwards she was given a drink and a few words exchanged about how she felt, and how the sickness and 'coming up'[5] feeling would pass. The older women in the queue knew how to calm her down having been in that position themselves at some point in their clubbing and drug taking careers. The women's toilets are also seen as a women-only space, where you can go and chat or 'chill out' (they are large in this particular club). Occasionally the odd man may appear in search of a missing partner. This is tolerated, but any man who stays in the space creates a feeling that a 'sacred' place has been invaded. One informant said of such an incident 'doesn't he know this is our place, he shouldn't be here'. There was also a feeling of disapproval

---

is often used in North America and Europe to describe all forms of electronic dance music. (http://en.wikipedia.org/wiki/Techno_music)

5   The term 'coming up' refers to the feeling of euphoria or rush that comes over clubbers when the ecstasy pills they have taken start to have an effect. For some people this 'coming up' sensation is very uncomfortable involving nausea and/or vomiting, although this depends on a number of issues such as the amount taken, and what other substances ecstasy has been mixed with.

towards the woman he was with, that she had broken an unspoken rule. The level of tolerance and the relaxed attitudes in this club space can be summed up in the following quote: 'They just seemed less frantic, it seemed less about doing drugs, much more relaxed' (Diane).

A Mainstream Club Night

The second type of club experience described is not as friendly and is a space that has a different atmosphere. This impression is given on entering the club and being in the space itself as there is none of the communal atmosphere described in the previous account. The event is much larger and nearer the 'corporate'[6] club image, in terms of the music and dress and of the people attending, who are younger (approximately seventeen to twenty five years).

At the door the bouncers are large, intimidating and in traditional bouncer uniform; black 'puffa' jackets and trousers. They control the number of people going in and watch cash transactions carefully. Guest lists are fraught with hassle and claims to be on the list often have to be verified with the aid of the person sponsoring entry on the list. The stairs to the first floor are littered with various groups of clubbers trying to 'chill out'. The room on the first floor is frenetic with bodies jumping around; very hot and sweaty with loud 'hardcore'[7] music, with a high number of beats per minute. There is a squash round the bar and the cloakroom with people taking as many drugs as possible as soon as possible.

The second floor of the club has seats and slightly less hardcore music with fewer beats per minute. But even here the atmosphere is still chaotic and a bit fraught. Drug use is a mixture of amphetamine, ecstasy and cocaine; dancing to 'hardcore' music makes this a necessity. Those who attend tend to be much more 'on one' intent on 'losing it'.[8] Therefore the dance floor can get very unpleasant with no friendliness and some aggression. The harder music and more aggressive attitude was summed up by Jackie 'I think I found the atmosphere was more aggressive, I always felt more edgy and not quite as safe as I did in (names club). I think it was because the music was aggressive that it gives it more of an aggressive atmosphere' (Jackie).

The crowd who attend this club night are much younger and narrower in terms of style and *attitude*. Fashion is really important with all the best trainers, T-shirts on

---

6   In using 'corporate' to describe a club event the term refers to large gatherings or club nights, that are seen to make a profit, or which are seen to be only out to make a profit. This is seen as a negative thing by the female clubbers presented in this book. They are like a corporate business in that they have large financial resources. It is also corporate clubs that tend to have dress codes, high prices and cater for a mainstream audience.

7   Hardcore is a term that refers to a particular type of techno music that has a high number of beats per minute.

8   These terms describe a more single-minded attitude towards taking drugs, being in as much of an altered state as possible with little or no interaction with others attending the evening.

show, and women in trendy club wear, strappy dresses and shoes. People tend to feel out of place if not dressed up to some extent. Women occasionally get hassle from the younger men for looking different with tattoos and piercings, and being obvious with a same sex partner is not advisable. The atmosphere in this space is not as open or tolerant of people who are different.

The people who attend are socially different to those on the previous *underground* scene described earlier. In this more 'corporate' club scene people come from outside Manchester to club and they tend to come into Manchester to have a blow out and get as 'off their heads' as possible in a short space of time.[9]

The women's toilets are also a different experience to that described in the previous account. There is no friendly chatting and smiles are met with cool stares. Anyone who stumbles a bit or looks a bit ropey is ignored, and the feeling seems to be a very unsympathetic 'if you can't take it don't do it', or that it is uncool to be unable to handle drink or drugs.

Diversity and Clubbing Experiences

It is apparent that women describe their experiences of 'being on the scene' differently according to the kind of club space being referred to. This can be understood in terms of the extent to which clubbing has been incorporated into the mainstream. Collin (1997) charts the rise of gangland violence associated with the boom in clubbing in Manchester. Around 1993 'Madchester' became 'Gunchester' which spelt disaster for many of the larger focal spaces for clubbing. The Criminal Justice and Public Order Act 1994 also had an impact on clubbing in Manchester. It came into force at a time when clubs were suffering from gang intimidation and violence and had the effect of driving 'rave' into controlled venues, towards the mainstream, into a wider community. What was originally intended as an alternative to the mainstream generated a new mainstream; the high street dance culture 'Mainstream house clubbing, with its closed circuit security cameras, registered door staff and council imposed procedural guidelines, had become the regulated opposite of its illicit origins' (Collin 1997, 268).

So in Manchester while there are still bigger more 'mainstream' clubs operating smaller more innovative nights have grown in number. These smaller more innovative club nights can be seen as the new undergrounds as they evolved as a reaction to the regulations of the Criminal Justice and Public Order Act 1994, and to the violence and intimidation happening in clubs such as the 'Hacienda', 'Home' and 'Sankey's Soap'. These diverse spaces offer clubbers a much more varied choice in terms of music, venue and crowd attending. Although *undergrounds* can be acknowledged as a problematic term, as *mainstreams* tend to swallow them up, in Manchester it is clear that there are distinct levels or hierarchies of club spaces with women clearly

---

9   There can be differences between mainstream club spaces, usually depending on the size of the event, the larger the event the more 'out of town' and younger the crowd is likely to be

identifying with one type or another. This emphasizes the importance of difference and the concept of *undergrounds* and *mainstreams*. As 'Gail' described it 'I think you can see it (clubbing) going from underground to mainstream and then all these other little offshoots spark up and they're the sort of underground.'

There is evidence from female clubbers and promoters to suggest that in Manchester club scenes were seen as going through a fallow period in the late 1990s. The closure of some of the big name clubs such as the 'Hacienda', 'Home' and 'Sankey's Soap' from 1994–1997 is perceived as having started the decline.[10] In the words of Jessica a clubber and promoter:

> The scene is very much split and fragmented and with the closure of things like 'Sankey's' and 'Kaleida'. The scene when it first started off was small then there was a mushrooming of the scene, now there seems to be a switch to bars and eateries and it's a case of the rave generation growing up. For promoters it's a case of where do you put on a night?
>
> (Jessica)

Other promoters of club nights disagreed with this view and felt that the scenes had changed but not too much, and that neither had it 'slowed up'. The different club nights on offer could be a factor currently contributing to the success of club scenes. In the view of club promoters the move has had to be away from large venues into smaller more underground clubs. As 'John' another promoter put it:

> The music has changed, and the audience, but not that much. People who go out to dance clubs now are just going through the same motions that we went through when it started. I remember it was really kicking in clubs and warehouses in Manchester ten years ago and it still is but in different places.
>
> (John)

So for 'John' clubbers are engaging in the same types of behaviour as they were ten or fifteen years ago, they are just doing it in different types of spaces. The way in which the changing relationship of clubbing to bar based socialising contributes to this diversity in the city is described by 'Jackie':

> The thing with Manchester is that bars have taken over now. That's why all the clubs are clearing out. There's so many bars that have late licenses it's like, what's the point of going to a club you don't have to, (names place) is open until two and plays dance music.
>
> (Jackie)

The direction that club nights have taken in diversifying was also highlighted by female clubbers. The prevalence of the 'corporatization' of clubs was particularly mentioned. The experience of corporate clubs was seen to be much less satisfying as they were perceived as an uninteresting package with a routine formula. 'Ruth' described this as a 'loss of meaning' because:

---

10 'Sankey's Soap' reopened in 2000

It has got a certain shallowness to it and the more commercial it gets the less meaningful it's becoming. I don't necessarily like the posiness that goes with the idea of the culture around it, the clothes you're wearing and the image you're supposed to keep up, the designer label thing has taken over quite a lot and I don't like that.

(Ruth)

More innovative spaces or 'free parties' were seen as much more exciting, unpredictable and fun, contrasted with the 'soullessness' of mainstream experiences. As illuminated in the following quotes from the data, women clubbers recognized these differences.

I know mates who would go out to (names club) on a Saturday night and you'd ask them how it was – 'oh okay'. But that's taking drugs in a mainstream environment there's no intrigue. I used to like the seediness of going to free parties to take it and it used to be there all the time. Now it's we buy our drugs on Tuesday to be ready for Saturday, to go out and pretend we're having a lovely time to Ibiza tunes and all go home together. It's so boring and there's nothing to go on to afterwards to have all those fun nights and meet new people.

(Alice)

It's kind of summed up in that they (Es) used to be called doves then they were called Mitsubishis, that's how corporate it is!

(Jackie)

Some club spaces attempt to recreate the atmosphere of old style 'raves'. These tend to be larger, more 'one off' events with the space to do so. 'Sheila' described the experience of such an event as:

It was just a real experience, so different from a night club because the people who organize it make a real effort to make the place look nice and comfortable. The atmosphere was friendly and wandering through all these rooms was a multi-sensual experience. It was very different from the traditional night club where you've got men leering at women on the dance floor.

(Sheila)

'Being on the Scene'

It is apparent through women's involvement on club scenes that different kinds of club spaces are significant and that along with different venues to choose from clubbing women defined the kind of music played as a deciding factor in where to go out, and recognized that this varied from night to night. Music is often seen as unimportant to women, as DJ-ing is produced as a 'male' occupation and female clubbers are seen as being passive and uninvolved in the essence and production of club spaces. Female clubbers are also seen as opting out of competing with men by not taking an interest in music (Thornton 1995). However, this is challenged by the women clubbers presented here, where music emerges as an important factor in identifying with a particular scene or scenes. Music as well as drug use is of the utmost importance in allowing consumers to express themselves through dance:

> A crowd which dances to house music is bound on a route to pure escape, whilst at the same time celebrating a sense of community which has been forged at the moment of interactive consumption. It is therefore of major importance that a crowd is able to 'gell' together.
>
> (Reitveld 1998, 189)

For female clubbers if the music was not right, the night was not either. Women clubbers felt the music was important to them, although their reasons for this were different. Some were interested in specific DJs and referred to themselves as 'spotters',[11] while others felt a particular type of music made their night 'right'. This is reflected in the following responses:

> I prefer consistency and continuity, I don't like clubs that have good slots of music and then they'll suddenly change it to something else unrelated which disturbs your mood. It's really important to me, music, and it can make or break your night
>
> (Diane)

> I quite like a mixture of music actually, but I'm not into really bad transitions. I like seeing bands in clubs as well, it's nice to have a focus on things rather than non-stop endless dancing.
>
> (Gail)

Music was also important to female clubbers as it was linked to pleasure and dancing. Within some club spaces coded as 'safe' this pleasurable act of dancing could be indulged in without fear of harassment from men. In the context of club spaces, a sense of bliss is associated with the intenseness of dancing, as sexuality and identity are intricately linked, and it is this that has led some writers to suggest that club spaces offer a 'safe' alternative to sexual activity and intercourse (see Henderson 1996; McRobbie 1994). However, 'safe' in this clubbing context is problematic because of difference as not all spaces used for clubbing necessarily offer women safer spaces to perform sexualities. A sense of self is certainly altered or changed in 'losing it' on the dance floor and this is exactly what attracts women to the temporary communities within club spaces. Clubbing women agreed that interaction on the dance floor is not uncommon and through this difference is revelled in and 'tribal' associations confirmed. So difference is emphasized, not lost, in some club spaces as clubbers define through difference, who belongs where.

The different types of music played attract different people, so music choice for women is linked to *attitude*. The 'right' sort of people will congregate with the 'right' *attitude* in spaces where certain music is played, although this is subjective as

---

11 This term refers to women who are interested in particular DJs and genres of music. They tend to have a wide ranging knowledge of dance music and will look out for or 'spot' DJs that interest them.

different women enjoy different atmospheres and music styles. This was not only the case from the consumers' point of view; promoters' of club nights felt the same.

> My diversity started with this scene. (names club) was the start of it really and doing the opposite to everyone else. We do world music nights, dub nights, breakbeat, trance, and they're all off the wall and breaking the boundaries of dance music.
>
> (John/promoter)

As *attitude* is so important to women's participation in club spaces, they pay special attention to recommendations on where to go from friends who have experienced particular events. Also club promoters seem to realize the importance of this 'nurturing' of a specific crowd, with flyers being given out in particular places that are designed to attract such a crowd. However it is not just DJs that attract people to club spaces, it can be the promoters themselves, as party organizations can become just as renowned as the DJs themselves (Rietveld 1998). John's a club promoter from Manchester and his organization is well known for putting on club nights, and the fact that they are behind various club nights influences peoples' choice of what spaces to visit.

Issues such as decor and comfort were mentioned by respondents as affecting the atmosphere and *attitude* within club spaces. Access to water, heat levels and 'chill out' spaces were mentioned as safety factors and therefore as necessary to enjoying a club night. The lighting and décor of club spaces were important in creating 'atmosphere':

> The most important requirement of club and party lighting is that 'normal' visual perception of space is ruptured in a way that pleases or amuses the crowd, so that the tactile and acoustic space created by a loud sound system with a sensuous bass sound is accentuated.
>
> (Reitveld 1998, 172)

Therefore small, pokey, grim, large spaces can be transformed by attention to lighting and décor. The Hacienda's theme nights such as 'HOT' in which the club was transformed into a 'beach' with sunny yellow lighting, a small pool, and props such as beach balls (Reitveld 1998), is an example of this kind of transformation. For female clubbers this type of effort was seen in a positive way, and club spaces that were seen to put no effort into their surroundings were avoided.

A number of female clubbers identified hierarchies or groups within the scenes themselves. The following quotes are explicit about the fact that there are exclusive 'hip' groups within Manchester club scenes. These 'hip' spaces tend to exclude women on the basis of 'subcultural capital' (Thornton 1995). Men within club spaces are seen as possessing subcultural capital in the form of music knowledge, being a DJ, promoter, bouncer, or having the 'right' sort of attractive girlfriend. For women clubbers their subcultural capital is based on their ability to 'fit in' to a particular scene and is based around their sexuality and physical attractiveness. It could be parts of a social grouping as 'Anne' suggests:

I think the scene can be quite exclusive certainly. I suppose within every part of life there's cliques that exist ... in Manchester within such a small environment if you do go to any parties that are VIP it's always the same faces that are at the same free dos.

(Anne)

'Cynthia' outlines the fact that in attending a club night where she would not 'fit in', the analysis of her by those who do belong, would see her as 'unhip' and at the bottom of that particular hierarchy:

If I were to drop into (names club) I'd stick out like a sore thumb, not being six stone, fifteen and going out in my underwear. Different types of clubs and different types of music, it tends to be split off into loads of different crowds and I think people can easily identify who their pack members are. I think it's definitely a gang mentality.

(Cynthia)

Therefore 'subcultural capital' is a 'currency which legitimizes the unequal statuses' (Thornton 1995, 104). It is young women and not young men who are looked upon with derision if they appear out of context in club scenes, supporting the argument that to be 'unhip' is an intrinsic female characteristic, linked to the expression of female sexuality. 'Jessica' highlights the importance of difference in terms of style:

If you go to (names club) and look at the women there, you're going to find more fashion victims and less hippies, but you do get a mixture in clubs, but it's specific to certain types of clubs and they're smaller nights, as you move into the corporate clubbing thing you get more uniform.

(Jessica)

The Attraction of Club Spaces for Women

Given the diversity of spaces for clubbing in terms of music, style, attitude and location what was the attraction of different spaces for female clubbers and what made them choose a particular venue over others? Where to go clubbing was decided by a variety of means that were interrelated. For women clubbers, the main persuading factor was a recommendation from a friend, but music was also important as it had a bearing on other factors linked to the club space. Important factors in choosing where to go are illuminated by 'Gail' and 'Diane' as:

A combination of all those (flyers, music, venue, DJs, people who go, word of mouth) but predominantly music because whatever you're into attracts the sort of people you want to be there.

(Diane)

I think if you heard about a club, but also heard it was really dodgy, it would put me off. So a combination if someone's been there before and said it was really good.

(Gail)

Many clubs and promoters produce flyers to advertise their club nights and to attract clubbers. Flyers were mentioned by female clubbers as important but mainly because they were not seen as being very good or well designed. A few good ones that stood out were highlighted but mainly there was a consensus amongst female clubbers that clear, concise information was what was needed.

> I just want to know what the club night is, where it is, who's playing, how much it is and how late the bar is open till. Specific places have specific flyers, (names record shop) has all the techno nights and maybe it's where you hang out and where you pick up flyers that relates to who they attract.
>
> (Alice)

Women clubbers felt that, in general, promoters aimed their nights at specific groups of people, so the whole package of venue, music, price and crowd who attended were right for the group it was aimed at. Women clubbers could be put off going to club nights for a variety of reasons; high prices, queues, the bar closing early, staggered prices depending on the time you arrive. The only thing that female clubbers emphasized that needed changing, were the attitudes of security staff who were seen as 'hassling' people for no reason. The attitude of security towards people using cannabis was seen as 'over the top', when there were others in the club who were being aggressive due to alcohol consumption.

> The only thing that annoys me is over zealous security. In general they are unfriendly, thuggish and always seem to be picking on the wrong people. You don't want to be kicked out for skinning up,[12] you want them to sort out the pissed bloke giving everyone grief.
>
> (Theresa)

Therefore the attitude of security staff was a huge issue for women who went clubbing. This, if it were negative, would persuade them to steer clear of particular club nights even if it was perceived as a good night out in other ways. Bouncers working at mainstream clubs were seen to be the worst culprits, as the following quote reveals.

> The only place I remember the security staff being really obnoxious was (names club), it completely put me off going there. They had a female security officer that would come and look underneath the toilet doors and be really out of order.
>
> (Gail)

Sexuality and perceptions of sexuality by others that attended the club night were also important in deciding where to go. It was important to clubbing women that others who attended the places they went to, had open minds towards different sexualities and alternative expressions of femininity. The question of differences in attitudes towards women in particular club spaces, was seen as vital to a good night, and was an influencing factor in deciding where to go. Women clubbers preferred

---

12 This is a slang term that refers to rolling a joint with cannabis and tobacco.

nights where the sexual vibe was less apparent and where men were viewed as being more 'clued up' towards feminism, as 'Jackie' states:

> I think a lot are aware that 'no' means 'no' and the persistence of men isn't apparent, although it depends a lot on the clientele. In a lot of places we choose to go, the lads are a bit more aware of feminism.
>
> (Jackie)

Women clubbers identified mainly with one type of clubbing experience, but were also open to anything new and tended to describe themselves as 'dabblers', so their identities were changeable according to what sort of club space they were in. 'Gail' and 'Alice' emphasize that it is the diversity of club scenes that attracts them and other clubbers as this diversity means that there is a choice of music, style and drug use.

> I'm quite into trying different things, it depends on who's around, but I try to avoid going to the same place too often. I'm not always up for a heavy pilled-up night, I dabble.
>
> (Gail)

> I think my clubby outings might be on a celebratory scale for someone's birthday or it might just be an appreciation of a crowd of people. If a group of friends were going somewhere I wouldn't normally go, it's them that makes the vibe, so I'm a dabbler too.
>
> (Alice)

Club Spaces and Drugs

The use of illegal drugs such as ecstasy was seen as an integral part of the experience of female clubbers. They stated that on a personal level their drug usage had changed a great deal, but in club scenes overall it was still the case that people attending did an 'awful lot of drugs'. An interesting point to note is how clubbing women talked about the diversity of drugs used, and shifts in what were the primary drugs used. Drug use varied between club scenes, so participants' drug of choice, or attitudes towards drug use could exclude them from some spaces, and include them in others. The way of using drugs is also important, and illustrates some of the differences in behaviour between *mainstream* and *underground* clubbers. In some *mainstream* clubs the use of drugs can be more extreme and aggressive, leaving participants isolated. In other spaces, the *underground* clubs, drugs were used in a less aggressive way with an emphasis on friendliness and interaction, through the use of ecstasy. However according to female clubbers, the quality of ecstasy dropped in the mid to late 1990s, and cocaine became more available (Kilfoyle and Bellis 1998), which could have changed the ethos in some club spaces. As 'Diane' highlights:

> There was a real slump in the quality of ecstasy for ages, and then all of a sudden there were good drugs around again. I got really disillusioned with it because I kept getting crap drugs.
>
> (Diane)

Drug usage is also related to the presence of alcohol on club scenes as increasingly clubbers are polydrug users who consume a wide range of drugs in conjunction with each other and also in combination with alcohol. With this change in drug use came a change in the ethos of some clubs, with the emergence of 'new laddism', an aggressive masculinity and an emphasis on sex (Saunders 1997). The following quotes suggest some of the reasons why this change or shift in drug use may have occurred.

> You went out and took as many drugs as you possibly could and then drank until you collapsed! I think it's changed a lot, because there's a lot more coke about and it's cheap.
>
> (Alice)

> The thing is, a couple of years ago you really started to notice it (cocaine), it used to be a real luxury and now it's starting to get a lot more common. Maybe it's because we're all getting older and more affluent.
>
> (Gail)

However, the changes in drug use in club spaces, particularly the use of cocaine, highlights the importance of the use of drugs in the production of cultural spaces of consumption. The fact that cocaine use has become more prevalent in club spaces in Manchester has important effects on *attitude* within those spaces and consequences for the women who use them. A more aggressive, 'macho' attitude has been observed that affects how safe club spaces feel to women participating in them.

Some female clubbers expressed one of the down sides of clubbing as feeling a covert pressure to take drugs, and felt that for a small minority of people, drugs had a bad effect on their lives. This meant that for them, clubbing experiences were not all fun and had a serious side. As 'Naomi' observed:

> I did feel at first that there was quite a lot of pressure on me to take drugs which I resisted for quite a while. After a while it became clear to me there was a cliqueyness associated with the scene too, knowing the names of DJs, and the different types of music, and there was obviously a darker element to it, the promoters, the drug dealers and that could make me feel a bit nervous.
>
> (Naomi)

Other issues relating to clubbing and drug use concern appropriate behaviour towards others that is expected, especially by men towards women, and being aware that people had altered their mental state with the use of drugs. Clubbing women suggested the context of these social rules as:

> Don't shout about taking drugs, don't waltz into a club going 'has anybody got any E'; be cool, be sort of secretive even thought it's accepted that everybody's doing it, you know, be smart, be subtle, and if you broke that rule, people would think you were a real wanker. I would hope not sexually harassing people.
>
> (Sheila)

If you see someone sweating pass them your bottle of water, never say 'no' to passing anyone water. I think a lot of it is to do with behaviour, not being too imposing on people and understanding what stage of going up or going down they might be.

(Lucy)

Female clubbers found it hard to talk about the social rules that are associated with club spaces, but what they did say can be interpreted in terms of 'subcultural capital' and 'hipness' (Thornton 1995). In particular it was essential that clubbers did not come across as being naïve and uneducated about drugs, such as asking questions of strangers such as 'what have you had?' There were also forms of 'hipness' surrounding the dance floor. It was implicit that men did not harass women on the dance floor, and any men that did engage in this type of behaviour were cut off from any group dancing or friendly fun. Therefore there are gendered rules on club scenes that made this kind of behaviour 'uncool', and gender is important in negotiating style and behaviour in club spaces through adopting the right *attitude*. If men broke the social rules about behaviour and attitude, this would have consequences for them. For example, 'Sophie' described how:

You might get excluded from certain types of communal activity like dancing together, grabbing hold of each other, or showing each other bits of jewellery that glow. If someone's being a bit of a git you're just not going to communicate with them anymore.

(Sophie)

What is notable about particular social rules associated with club scenes is that female clubbers could not pin down exactly what these were and tended to answer in relation to *attitudes* instead of appearance for example. This was important to the way women within club scenes identified with others who attended the same events, and how clubbing women saw their own sexuality and identified with others who shared their sense of self was of the utmost importance. Women clubbers wanted to feel they were socialising with like-minded people and that they were not targets for harassment by men, as experienced in alcohol-based clubs for example. Therefore judging people on their *attitude* was crucial to determine whether they belonged, and adhered to the rules regarding women and sexual behaviour. Women clubbers stated they could distinguish people on the basis of the use of 'clubby' terms, but that being on club scenes was a whole package of language, social etiquette and style. However *attitude* was the number one defining factor in deciding how to tell whether people belonged, and *attitude* was experienced in terms of gender-appropriate behaviour. 'Sheila' defined it in the following way:

If you've got guys in there with an 'eyeing up the chicks' attitude you might think 'what are you doing here, it's not that sort of place', regardless of what they're wearing. (names club) was typical I walked past this table with two lads, they offered me some sweets! I mean you don't go to (names a different club) and a couple of lads offer you some sweets; they'll say 'nice tits' or something. So there's an attitude and they sussed me out too, as someone they could offer their sweets to.

(Sheila)

The distinctions drawn between different types of participants on different scenes are also constructed through the language used. Language usage is a location of the person on the scene. Certain words and phrases that female clubbers could think of were described as 'really naff' and tended to be used only in a humorous context, by those attending underground clubs. Others attending mainstream clubs were seen to take the clichés more seriously, and use them in a serious fashion. Statements about language by women clubbers highlights 'uncool' clichés, and the fact that clubbing terms can communicate feelings effectively.

> A lot of it is music orientated and Americanisms as well, but I can't think of any that I hear or use. No one I know really uses them – they're clichés like, bangin', sorted, largin' it, but I think that's the nice thing about people I know. They don't get sucked into the whole thing and just exist in a vacuum of club life, they have other things to do.
>
> (Chris)

> People you don't know will say 'are you having a good one?' It's such a simple question but it means so much, you say 'yeah nice one', it sums up a lot of things.[13]
>
> (Ruth)

The use of sexist language is argued to be a form of social control of women and teenage girls (Lees 1997). However, the language on club scenes that female clubbers described, was based either around humorous terms or music and drug use. It is significant that within the club spaces where female clubbers felt comfortable there was an absence of words to describe women in a stereotypical way, such as the term 'slag'. The language on club scenes revolves around the 'props' of the scenes such as drug use and safety, not with denigrating women.

The differences between club spaces meant that for those participating on different scenes the rules were changeable and this could be unexpected. *Undergrounds* and *mainstreams* had different social rules regarding drug use. *Undergrounds* were seen as a friendly, social space for taking drugs, but *mainstreams* were seen as being a much more isolating experience. This was related to the *attitude* of the people attending and the atmosphere created by the differing music styles. For others, certain behaviours were expected and if not forthcoming were detrimental to their evening. As 'Chris', an 'underground' clubber put it:

> I think you've just not got to act like an idiot! Club scenes are an alternative counterculture thing, and the clubs that I choose to go to are ones which respect that legacy. It's about not being dodgy if you're a man to women, not being slimy or doing dirty dancing. You can drink but not get aggressive, and I think now, people don't like drug casualties, 'cos with some of the older people it's like, 'seen it', 'done it'.
>
> (Chris)

---

13 This quote refers to the experience of taking ecstasy that is couched in terms of a simple phrase 'are you having a good one?' Which can mean are you having a good pill or a good high as well as 'are you having a good night', so it is a covert way of asking another clubber about their drug use.

Although in both *mainstreams* and *undergrounds*, being explicit about taking drugs was seen to be 'uncool':

> They would come across as someone quite naïve and although people are out clubbing, they don't particularly talk about their drug use to one another.
>
> (Anne)

For women clubbers, club scenes were and still are, something new different and exciting because of the way they are treated by men, as more equal and with more respect than on alcohol-based club scenes. This is one of the reasons women clubbers were drawn to club spaces and one of the reasons why they are still enjoyed. As 'Anne' reflects:

> The first time I went out clubbing I enjoyed it much more than being stuck in a pub, pissed. There is a level of control to it. As a woman I enjoyed the freedom of being able to go out to a club and it not be about men chatting you up.
>
> (Anne)

'Jessica' describes the experience as:

> The freedom, the illicit nature, to enjoy, to party. It was a tremendous mix of people that came from all different walks of life, got together, had a good time and let their hair down. With the effects of E you start talking to somebody and barriers go down. People mix in a way that is unheard of in a class-ridden society and a patriarchy like the one we live in. For people to lose those defences, chat and fool around is a great thing.
>
> (Jessica)

For women clubbers the experience of participating in club spaces was enjoyed because it was different from an aggressive alcohol-based culture.

> The first club I went to was the Hacienda and I just ended up chatting to people and it was a million miles away from that beer, lad culture that I'd previously experienced. There was a good vibe and it was relaxing and there was an emphasis on enjoying yourself that I found quite refreshing really, rather than getting tanked up to your eyeballs and seeing if you could get into a fight.
>
> (Naomi)

Or it was an integral part of a social life that they had always followed.

> Mainly I prefer to go out on the gay scene, as I'm bisexual and I think that's how I got into it, clubbing is a major part of gay life.
>
> (Lucy)

Dress Codes, *Attitude* and 'Feeling Right'

Another important aspect of *attitude* is style and how differences between groups of clubbers in terms of fashion can affect the atmosphere in club spaces and the experiences of clubbing women. When discussing style as part of identity on club scenes, women clubbers saw the different scenes in Manchester as clearly divided in terms of style, and this affected what types of nights they identified with and placed themselves within. They felt that some spaces for clubbing were much more to the fore and in the mainstream which meant some pubs and clubs had strict dress codes where casual wear was not acceptable. There was a general consensus that you had to look 'right' to fit in to different spaces and to also have the 'right' *attitude* to go with the look. Differences in the type of music played were seen to attract differing crowds of people with a specific style. As 'Alice' observed:

> Different music attracts different types of people like jungle obviously attracts different cultures, and techno attracts a young crowd and lots of baggy trousers; also lots of speed being used. (names club night) are a bigger more friendly crowd and (names club night) was more specifically a Mancunian club where it was local people.
>
> (Alice)

There was also a consensus that there was the right 'look' for the clubs attended and if you did not look 'right' you would not get in.

> A friend of mine tried to get into (names club), he was quite conventional looking but he loved clubbing and they wouldn't let him in. So he obviously didn't look right so maybe there are dress codes influencing whether people get in or not.
>
> (Sheila)

One of the main points highlighted when discussing fashion and style in relation to different club nights, was that of dress codes in clubs, and whether women clubbers felt constrained by them. Women at club events have been described as 'rave girls in hot pants and bra tops' (McRobbie 1994, 169). At the time of writing, McRobbie's description could be said to be representative of femininity at raves. However, club scenes have changed over time and this kind of highly sexualized dress code is not to be found everywhere. It is also looked down upon in some venues as being 'unhip' or 'uncool', as something to be held up as the stereotypical 'dolly' image of women. This had a significant bearing on whether or not women clubbers would attend a particular club night. In general the more *mainstream* and 'corporate' a club night, the stricter the dress code was, so style in these spaces is more regulated. Also in *mainstreams* attitudes to women were not as open as they were in more informal underground club spaces. This was seen as a worry for women who attended, in that they would not be taken seriously by men and be treated accordingly. 'Diane' illuminates objections to dress codes by stating she would not attend club spaces that operated these policies. This is due to a feeling that women are unnecessarily and unfairly treated by such policies, as female clubbers feel constrained by official club dress codes, in terms of femininity and having to fit themselves into a particular type of image that they objected to, but that was seen as appropriate by some clubs.

> I totally disagree with the whole dress code thing, to the extent that I wouldn't go anywhere that operated that door policy.
>
> (Diane)

I've never felt anywhere I've wanted to go 'oh fuck, I've got the wrong clothes on'. You don't want to go if you have to think 'what shall I wear to look right'.

(Gail)

One of the reasons why club scenes have been located so much to the fore of the mainstream is that legal regulation has encouraged commercialization and 'corporatization'. Club nights are just that. They happen within a designated area, with rules and regulations concerning opening times and licensing. Club nights are controlled by this very fact, and are also open to commercialized interests. This commodification of style (Hebdige, 1979), means the *undergrounds* and their challenges are incorporated into the mainstream via the 'trickle up' effect (Thornton 1995), and that what starts out as a challenge ends up in high street shops as the new mainstream, inevitably creating a new set of conventions. Although this commercialization and corporatization of club nights may have succeeded in driving some fashions, music styles, and clubs underground. The big 'corporate' clubs have dress codes, high prices and mainstream music, whereas the smaller nights that are surviving in Manchester have no official dress codes, reasonable prices and experimental DJs.

The consumption of club nights involves a whole package of music, atmosphere, style and the right kind of clothes. As club scenes became more commercialized and corporatized dress codes became routine in the mainstream clubs. Women clubbers stated that they could tell which types of people went where, by the way they dressed, and that in certain clubs they would expect certain groups to gather. Club fashion in some spaces works to the detriment of women involved, as it exploits and constrains them in forcing conformity to restricting images of femininity. Gender inequalities may operate within club spaces, if women are trivialized as 'babes'. Specific to this 'babe' image are the symbolic meanings given to sexualized, emphatic clothing, so women are looked upon as the 'other', and then marginalized as 'unhip' in terms of 'subcultural capital'. This is especially true of the more glamorous 'dollybird' fashion, which involved high heels, short skirts and tight tops. Although women clubbers felt there had been a rebellion against this type of image. As 'Ruth' put it:

It went through a backlash, the whole kind of 'babe' image of wearing short skirts, high heels, glittery this, quite a lot of women decided it was more comfortable to go out in trainers, so there's a constant change in what is fashionable and what people will put up with, 'cos you can only put up with wearing uncomfortable clothes for so long!

(Ruth)

Women clubbers often subvert mainstream 'glamorous' clothing by emphasizing or de-feminizing different articles of clothing and in doing so challenge and resist traditional signifiers of femininity. By resisting in this way, female clubbers subvert the feminized 'unhip' image of female clubbers by using style in an ironic way, and any hostile male *attitude* is confused by the subverted image, and stereotypical images of women are thrown back for re-examination. As for 'Chris' in the quote below, her performance of her sexuality suggests contradicting aspects of femininity and these contradictions are pleasurable to her, due to their ironic nature.

> I used to wear quite outrageous stuff, PVC, rubber, but I did it in an ironic way, with huge boots, and obviously having very short hair made it kind of jar.
>
> (Chris)

The 'Riot Grrl' movement also engaged in a similar type of subversion of the 'other'. The women involved in this specifically female scene challenged notions of female display by writing words such as 'slut' and 'whore' on their bodies. This labelling of themselves pre-empted any derogatory comments that may have been directed at them. It directly confronted the viewer with terms designed to prohibit female display (Leonard 1997). Parodies of traditional gender images also undermine societal claims of a naturalized set of gender identities (Butler 1990), and it is this notion of a rigid, narrow performance of gender and femininity that women within club spaces are attempting to avoid. In occasionally moving from space to space within club scenes and having to look or perform differently within each space, it means that for female clubbers their identities are not fixed and permanent, and that this is a source of pleasure for the women clubbers concerned. This movement between spaces can be seen as being from *undergrounds* to *mainstreams* and vice versa, although this is quite rare, as women tended to identify either with *mainstreams* or *undergrounds*. Movement can also be seen to take place between the different spaces of *undergrounds* or *mainstreams*, as even within these two categories there are subtle differences in style, performance of gender and *attitude*.

Identities through similar styles of clothing were seen to be more meaningful to participants in *undergrounds* rather than *mainstreams*. Wearing certain types of clothes such as combat trousers, fleeces or certain designer labels sent out signals to others that you were on their level, part of the group and on 'the same wavelength'. Although what are seen to be underground clubs operate no official dress code, female clubbers stated that they would feel out of place if they did not fit in with the general style. Consumption in different club scenes is divided in worlds of style and fashion, with some clubs being out of bounds for feeling comfortable for some women, due to the sorts of dress codes women were expected to conform to. This was expressed by 'Gail' as:

> There's towny clubbers and normal clubbers and you could divide normal clubbers into a million different categories as well. The towny dance scene I avoid like the plague 'cos it makes me feel uncomfortable and I don't feel like I'm one of them. The give away for me is walking through Manchester late at night and the women are wearing very short negligee-type outfits with strappy sandals and not very many other clothes!
>
> (Gail)

As highlighted in chapter 1 there have been changes in the way that society is organized and one of these changes is argued to be a significant shift in the perception of lifestyles and subcultural groupings. Lifestyles as part of group identity and belonging were thought of as fixed sets of tastes and leisure practices that set different groups apart. Now, it could be argued that contemporary lifestyles are more actively formed, in which coherence and unity give way to an exploration of more transitory experiences (Featherstone 1990). The divisions within different club scenes are an example of these changes as female clubbers do not confine themselves to experiencing only one type of clubbing event, but may sample many in their clubbing careers, defining and redefining their identities as they cross from one to the other.

Female clubbers also felt the diverse scenes had produced groups who were very tribal in style and dress as the following quotes in relation to underground nights illuminate. The dress code is not an official one as official dress codes are implemented when the club provides rules regarding style of dress, and not conforming means that clubbers will not gain entry. 'Unofficial' dress codes are less easy to define, but generally those attending will wear similar clothes, and if someone deviates from the norm and portrays a 'dolly' image for example, they may be looked upon with amusement or scorn. Women clubbers not only identified with one particular 'scene', but also could adapt for different 'scenes' if they wished to. However all clubbing women had their favourite nights and dressed accordingly to be part of it.

> There are women with piercings and I've got tattoos, so I think its a chicken and egg thing – is it because you're different that you do it, or is it doing it that makes you different? People on the scene generally care less about what society's stereotypes are and less about conforming to them. Though they care less about mainstream stereotypes there is a tribal thing, you've got your fluffy bras and strappy heels, your hippy type with piercings, your old school baggy pants, absolutely it's very tribal.
>
> (Jessica)

'Jessica' states that groups of people can be identified within particular club spaces and attributed to certain 'tribes'. In terms of the movement of clubbing women from *mainstreams* to *undergrounds*, and vice versa membership of overlapping groups means that social status and identity become ambiguous (Maffesoli 1996). Female clubbers tended to identify themselves as being involved in *undergrounds*, but occasionally they moved to participate in *mainstreams* for various reasons such friend's birthdays, or when others chose where to socialize. Therefore in doing what they describe as 'dabbling' they are participating in overlapping, 'tribal' groups albeit on a temporary basis.

This chapter has focused on issues surrounding why female clubbers are attracted to and participate in specific types of club spaces. The next chapter moves the book in a different direction and explores questions surrounding how club spaces are produced. How do female producers experience the worlds of drug dealing, DJ-ing and club promoting and how do they strive to find a place in the night time economy? These questions form the basis of the next chapter which examines the experiences of female producers of club spaces.

Chapter 3

Negotiating the Night Time Economy; Women as Drug Dealers, DJs and Club Promoters

Introduction

The production of club spaces in terms of DJ-ing, promoting and drug dealing is often a neglected area of study. This is in spite of the fact that DJs such as 'Sasha' for example have risen from 'relative anonymity to the status of international pop superstars' (Haslam 2002, 53). Female producers of club spaces contribute to the informal night time economy in a number of ways as DJs, promoters and as drug dealers. Therefore the purpose of this chapter is to analyse and explore the experiences of women who take part in the production of club spaces as part of the night time economy. These experiences are often ignored which begs the question 'why'? As is the case for female consumers of club spaces it is assumed that women who are involved in production through DJ-ing and promoting will be treated in a more equal way than those 'outside' these cultural industries (Milestone and Richards 1999). The same 'luved up', liberal attitudes are seen to permeate the business side of clubbing. However in a similar way to their female counterparts who consume club spaces, female DJs and promoters face discrimination and an uphill battle for recognition and respect from their male colleagues. For female drug dealers their contribution to the production of club spaces is often hidden, and it would be naïve to suggest that a similar 'luved up' attitude permeated their business activities. So whilst they also inhabit the night time economy they have to negotiate it in a different way. The fact that drug dealing is an illegal business activity has some bearing on the power hierarchies and masculine culture that are part of the drug dealer's illicit world. This chapter explores some of the reasons for the marginalization of women as club promoters, DJs and drug dealers.

Drug Dealing

One of the most important people on club scenes is the drug dealer and this data from one of the few women drug dealers in Manchester seeks to establish how other, male, dealers treated her: was there a gender bias in her client group, and how did she manage to cope in this very 'macho' male world of dealing? Whilst by no means

exhaustive in terms of data because of the difficulties of ethnography in this field, the analysis of her account of dealing can be understood with reference to Thornton's (1995) work regarding hierarchies within subcultural groupings. This area, the dealing of drugs, is under researched in general and almost nothing has been researched in the area of gender and drug dealing.[1] The malestream research that has been conducted around clubbing and drugs often denies women a place as thinking consumers, never mind as major operators behind the scenes. The purpose of this discussion of drug dealing and gender is to illuminate this under researched area of criminology. As the focus of this book is to discuss the gendered nature of the experiences of women related to club scenes, women who contribute to the night time economy in terms of business, both licit and illicit, are an important feature of these scenes. So this study of a female drug dealer focuses on how she negotiates the male world of drug dealing and its associated hierarchies. It is an exploration of the effects of gender on interactions in this hidden world which is part of the night time economy that is related to club spaces.

So what does 'Melanie's'[2] position as a drug dealer say about women who offend and can her experiences be related to theoretical frameworks and discussions regarding female criminality? Female criminality remains an under-researched area[3] and studies of female criminals commonly assume that women's crimes reflect their place in society and that they commit crimes, such as shoplifting, low level fraud and prostitution. However, illicit business women in the informal economy is an under-researched area and women have rarely been considered in this context. Criminal women often express values or objectives that may also be expressed by male criminals, although at the same time it is undeniable that their criminal careers are linked to their life experiences, that are specifically gendered (Carlen and Christina, 1985). It is also the case that traditional explanations for female crime do not recognize that money is just as much of a motivating factor for women who commit crime as it is for their male counterparts. So, although the female drug dealer discussed here is motivated in part by her dependency on amphetamines she is also focused on making money to support this habit, *as well as* a lifestyle that offers her a standard of living that would be unattainable otherwise. 'Melanie' has made a rational choice in making the decision to enter the arena of drug dealing (Davies, 1999). Therefore in looking at female criminality an over reliance on 'grand theory' is not possible. 'Grand theory' denies the complexity of individual experience and relies too heavily on notions of 'masculine' and 'feminine', without denying that criminality is undoubtedly linked to gendered social positions (Brown 1998). The experiences of 'Melanie' show that this particular type of criminality is very much affected by the gendered position of female drug dealers. In order to contextualize

---

1   With the notable exception of Denton and O'Malley (1999), Denton (2003).

2   Respondents naves been changed to ensure confidentiality

3   Naffine (1997) argues that criminology is still a discipline dominated by men and that its subject matter is also male dominated. She states that 'criminology is mainly about academic men studying criminal men and, at best, it would appear that women represent only a specialism, not the standard fare' (Naffine 1997, 1).

this discussion drug dealing can be considered as located within a distinct subcultural world of meanings and interactions, underpinned by the concept of 'hegemonic masculinity' (Connell 1995). Hegemonic masculinity is the culturally accepted form of masculinity that is desired over all others, although it is argued that differences and relations between masculinities must also be recognized. A particular type of hegemonic masculinity underpins criminal activities, stressing toughness, machismo, aggression and smartness (Brown 1998). In the cultural setting of drug dealing this is the accepted masculine ideal; to be tough, aggressive and smart.

Those involved in drug dealing have 'chosen' this particular 'career' because of the limited options that are available to them in terms of lifestyle choices. Assessment of risk is a major factor involved in this lifestyle choice, as are decisions about trust and safety. Gender is not only a signifier of risk in a world where female dealers suffer intimidation because of their gender it also affects how risk is negotiated in this particular social world. Trust is imperative for women involved in this drug dealing lifestyle, and gender also affects how trust is negotiated. Therefore the relationships surrounding drug dealing are constructed in terms of power. Female dealers who lack power in these relationships are still able to engage in behaviour that is empowering to them by 'getting back at' more powerful dealers who cause them problems. 'Melanie' talked about dealing as a business activity and the risks involved in such an activity, and did not refer to it as an act of rebellion or a political lifestyle choice. For her drug dealing was not about rebellion or a political ideal or statement, it is about money, not style, or music, but how to earn a good living. Therefore, drug dealing as a subculture needs to be looked at in a different way. As post-subcultural theorists (Bennett 1999; Muggleton 2000) suggest previous accounts of subcultural form and politics are not relevant to contemporary accounts of drug dealing. The boundaries involved in the complex hierarchies surrounding drug dealing are not fixed and shift according to changes in who has power over others. These boundaries therefore vary in different contexts based on interactions determined by gender. Networks of trust are also important for those involved in drug dealing as trusted contacts can be relied on if drug dealers need to call on reinforcements or aid if those further up the hierarchy attempt to put unwanted pressure on particular dealers. Kin and kin-type relationships were seen as central for women drug dealers (Denton and O'Malley 1999), and as these relationships were seen to be invaluable to women dealers it is interesting that 'Melanie' appeared to be very much on her own. Although she did have a kin-type relationship with a larger male dealer, and a close contact or friend within the brothel that she sold drugs into. These networks and relationships of trust also seem to be determined in some way by gender and status, as 'Melanie' is hindered by other more powerful dealers involved in a group from which she is excluded.

The subcultural world of dealing has its own hierarchies and sets of values and rules that must not be broken. 'Melanie', just by being a woman, seemed to break all the rules and had to deal accordingly with other people's reactions and attitudes. One of the questions for a woman as a drug dealer is how her gender affects the levels of risk associated with interactions with customers, suppliers and law enforcement agencies. As 'Melanie' recounts, female dealers in drugs encounter difficulties in establishing their own space of activity, and face opposition from other dealers.

> I used to get shit off this one person in particular, who didn't like anyone else selling, especially a 'girlie', which he made quite apparent.
>
> (Melanie)

This is made more difficult because of the hostilities they face as women. Melanie is very clear on the impact of this on her activities:

> With the guys, if you're a woman selling drugs, they just seem to be twice as defensive about it, as if you're stepping over from your territory into theirs. It seems it makes them feel more threatened than if it was another guy who started selling. They'd just have it out and it would be who ever did the best deals, did all right. I've tried not to be intimidated a bit by some people. It's not said (referring to threats) it's blatant really.
>
> (Melanie)

This hostility finds expression in a number of ways. The following quote refers to an incident with a customer. 'Melanie' was the frontline contact here as her workers were unavailable. This male customer assumes that they have gone away and left her in charge. It does not occur to him that she is *their* boss

> In the way that they'll obviously try and scam you they're saying they could because you're a girl and you're stupid and you don't know what you're doing, as if to say what do you think you're doing! He said 'I can't believe (names worker) has left you in charge', but I just thought 'you stupid idiot, it's me that's been doing it all along!'
>
> (Melanie)

It is not enough to view female drug dealers as victims and as marginalized in the illicit business economy. Although female dealers have their problems within the 'macho' dealing world, they are able to cope with them effectively in an intelligent way. Female dealers are able to gain some satisfaction in settling their business affairs in a way that 'gets one over' on suppliers who cause them problems. Women can be powerful and have agency in the hidden economy of dealing drugs even though they are affected by gender power relationships which they have to negotiate and make concessions to. Female dealers can 'play the game' or negotiate in the hegemonic masculine world of dealing despite being excluded as the female 'other' lacking in subcultural capital. The inequalities and constraints experienced because of her gender are illuminated in the account 'Melanie' gives of how she got started in dealing. Talking about how she established herself, she argued that it was not so much who supplied her as a dealer that was important and problematic, but how the dealing was financed, and by whom. As a woman she was undervalued by customers and suppliers, so to legitimize herself she had to pool her resources with an established male dealer and render herself invisible. When she was visible certain customers denigrated her and assumed that others were in charge. It simply did not occur to them that she was behind the whole operation. As she sums it up:

No, it's the people who you pool your money with, especially if they're already established and then you're seen as okay and it's acceptable. A lot of it depends on who you do business with yourself that carries a lot of weight.

(Melanie)

The financial arrangement was also of interest, as this could cause problems for 'Melanie' in the form of sudden price increases.

At first I was getting it on tick 'cos I was introduced to the person through a friend who backed me for credit, but then I tried to get the money together because it's cheaper, if you pay for it outright. But the person I get it off has started to put up the price so I've started pooling my money with someone else, so they had to drop the price because we're buying twice the amount in one lump, so they're suitably pissed off at the moment!

(Melanie)

This example illustrates that suppliers are in a position of power over buyers such as 'Melanie' who they see as weak. To gain power in this supplier/buyer relationship 'Melanie' had to pool her resources with a male dealer, who is more powerful in his relationship with the suppliers partly because he is male. 'Melanie' is powerless to force the supplier to put the price back down and does not have the resources to pay inflated prices. She also has less power in her relationship with the male dealer she pools her resources with and as a woman she is dependent on him to deal with the suppliers who cause her problems. He does not have the same problem so is not dependent on her in a similar way. Therefore her financial standing and credibility is a precarious one, based on a 'risky', stormy relationship with a bigger, more powerful, male dealer. This pooling of resources can be seen as a coping and protective strategy, but also as empowering to 'Melanie' as she feels she is 'getting one over' on the suppliers who harassed her. In carrying out interactions with customers, 'Melanie' as a female dealer is always conscious of her gender as a filter through which her reputation will be assessed. She has to learn to stand her ground and be assertive in a situation that may not come easily to her. 'Melanie' is taking a series of calculated risks and reinterprets her situation constantly in terms of how her customers, suppliers and society see her. Risk is not uniformly distributed throughout society and disadvantaged groups are therefore subject to more risk than others (Beck 1992). 'Melanie' is powerless against male intimidation and the threat of violence that accompanies her calculated risk as in this context her gender becomes a signifier of risk. She lacks the resources to threaten violence back and has to submit to unreasonable demands from suppliers. Violence is an issue that encroached greatly on 'Melanie's' life and was a source of stress and anxiety to her. It is recognized here that violence can be implicit and threatened as well as overt and physical. Physical violence does not have to occur for this to be a problem for 'Melanie', as the implication or threat that it could and would occur if she did not conform to the demands of more powerful dealers, is enough to make her feel anxious and unsafe. Therefore the 'risk' of being taken as a serious player is felt in the interactions 'Melanie' has with her supplier. When asked how suppliers treated her she retorts:

Oh take the piss!!! They take the piss which is why I've ended up in business with (names dealer) because they won't take the piss out of him. Another thing, if you always pay on time whenever they (suppliers) have financial difficulties they'll come to you for money. They (suppliers) came to me and said it would be fifty quid more (on the ounce). So now I let (names dealer) deal with them so I don't have to deal with them directly.

(Melanie)

So, what she is talking about is a form of robbery, based on intimidation and an implicit threat of violence. She is seen as an easy target due to her gender, and she is unable to defend herself against demands to pay more money. Here 'Melanie's' gender is significant as this makes her not only unusual enough to be highly visible, at least to her suppliers and other male associates, but it also makes her weak and vulnerable; the perfect target. Female drug dealers such as 'Melanie' need to develop strategies to protect themselves from male intimidation and threats of violence and one way that 'Melanie' does this is to make herself less visible by maintaining complex relationships with her 'workers'. Those who sold drugs on her behalf did not know about each other and it was assumed by those buying drugs that these men were in charge. This helped to lower 'Melanie's' visibility, at least in public, and meant that she did not have to cope with threatening behaviour in this arena. Her relationships with her 'workers' however followed the pattern of being based on conflict and mistrust and can be seen as 'risky' relationships. 'Melanie' seems to be a somewhat unusual case: the power and money behind a fairly large operation, but a heavy drug user, as it is usually the workers who are drug dependent and are consequently seen as risks to the business (Denton and O'Malley 1999). Women dealers were seen to be fewer than their male equivalents, but also less visible and this was seen as relating to the culture of masculinity that surrounds this illegal activity, the fact that a certain amount of 'front' and arrogance was seen to be needed to fulfil this role. 'Melanie' felt that the men who were involved in dealing cocaine were much more arrogant and visible, as they were happy to take on the role of the 'cool' person to score from, and that as a woman she did not feel as comfortable being that front person.

When I was doing the coke nobody knew it was me which was fine, but it seems like I do get off on the ego thing about it sometimes, and you can't help it, you get caught up in all that shit. I don't feel it's as important to me as it seems to be to every single guy that I've had dealings with who are willing to be quite blatant about the fact that they're the ones who are sorting it out because they are so cool!

(Melanie)

Within the world of dealing the problems of gender and being a woman do not stop at power relationships and threats of violence. Male counterparts withhold information and there is a feeling that women are not trusted as they will be weak if they get arrested. In reality it is probably less likely that a woman dealer will be arrested because she simply will not be suspected. However by the withholding of information and knowledge 'Melanie' is rendered invisible by male dealers and suppliers by being excluded from trust. This can be seen as a form of power brokering as, by withholding knowledge, these male dealers are demonstrating that they are more powerful.

> Not trusted as much with information and it becomes obvious when only so much is being said because you're there and you can either be sensitive about it and be paranoid or think 'fuck it' and let them think what they want.
>
> (Melanie)

An interesting question given that the world of drug dealing is dominated by hegemonic masculinity, is whether women as customers felt more comfortable buying drugs from another woman in the position of drug dealer, and whether 'Melanie' had more customers that were women than men.

> I think yeah but that's mainly because of working in the (names place), but if I don't include that, then it's about even, but it wasn't for a long time it was more women than men.
>
> (Melanie)

Male customers were seen as disliking buying drugs from a woman dealer as it put them in a subordinate position, and they would buy from almost anyone else. 'Melanie' was seen as a last resort because in such a male environment, the social rules for such an interaction were unknown and this put male customers off.

> I think a lot of it is status and the running about involved in dealing, and I think a lot of guys won't ask me for drugs. See women are fine about coming and asking me for stuff but a lot of guys don't like coming and asking me for drugs, and if they do it's as a last resort. They'd try everyone else first and me after.
>
> (Melanie)

Women customers were seen as less of a threat but also as more loyal, perhaps because they liked buying from a woman dealer and preferred not having to deal with men.

> I think part of it is because I started off selling to my mates, see if I was going to score drugs I would feel more comfortable if it was a woman, so the women customers I've got are more regular and constant. The thing is that you stay loyal to the person you score off and you'll always score off them if you can. That's more the women than the guys who it just doesn't matter as long as they score.
>
> (Melanie)

So, 'Melanie' is in a position where she feels that there are no legitimate lifestyles open to her. She feels marginalized by mainstream society because of her drug use, so involvement in the world of drug dealing is an area where she can wield power and validate her lifestyle choices. Her illegal route is a 'choice' based on low self-esteem and her individualized feeling of personal failing. The risk of being caught is a serious issue, but this risk is weighed up against the advantages of such a lifestyle. Contemporary society is increasingly perceived as characterized by risk and uncertainty which individuals are expected to negotiate on an individual level (Furlong et al. 1997). 'Melanie' expected that other legitimate means were not open to her, and even if they were they could not satisfy her lifestyle and her own drug habit. The level of risk in her life was high and negotiating it included a large amount of stress. However it was also linked to her self-esteem and confidence, so to take a high risk was worth it. She states that she uses dealing as a boost to her self confidence to validate herself, and this validation is linked to the uncertainty of the world she moves in.

> In passing but never seriously (talking about giving up drug dealing), because one, I couldn't afford to buy the amount I take if I wasn't selling and two, I've got used to the money that I do make from it, and also the lifestyle side of it. You do get hooked on the lifestyle side of it, you could say its easy money but it's not because if you get caught you're fucked. I think especially because I've never been a dead secure confident person I kind of thrive on feeling a little bit more important, I guess I use it for that to kind of validate myself a bit by it.
>
> (Melanie)

Therefore the gendering of production in terms of drug dealing means that 'Melanie' has to negotiate different obstacles to reach her goal of making money to support her own drug habit, and living the lifestyle she has chosen. One of these obstacles is the risk involved in such an activity that is taken on two different levels. The first is that it is an illegal activity and would carry heavy penalties if she was arrested. The second is the negotiating within the 'macho' dealing world that involves power brokering at every opportunity, and always having to battle to secure your 'product' at a reasonable price. As 'Melanie' herself states, due to her gender she is also excluded from important information as she is seen as a security risk in terms of the police, which means that she is not seen as one of a core group. The arguments surrounding drug dealing and gender are both complex and ambiguous as well as being under researched, although what can be concluded here is that for 'Melanie', risk is greater due to her visibility to other dealers and suppliers which is related to her gender. Also because of her gender, this directly impacts on the number of networks she can rely on and trust to back her up, hence the level of risk she takes is increased.

'Melanie's' position highlights that female offenders can be involved in a variety of crimes in ways similar to male offenders and that despite the risk, female drug dealers can be very successful in running this type of illegitimate business. They are powerful but hidden figures. 'Melanie' is influential and has negotiated her way into a powerful position, whilst not presenting a visible persona to the rest of the dealing world. Police statistics and previous limited research tends to illuminate female dealers who are both highly visible and desperate due to their own drug use, and that these are not necessarily the types of women who are influential in the drug dealing world (Denton and O'Malley 1999). Certain key issues emerge for 'Melanie', and for other female dealers, which can be summed up as involving risk and uncertainty, self-esteem and self-confidence, and exclusion and power. These are all issues that are involved in dealing drugs from a female perspective. To be a woman and a drug dealer carries a double risk: the need to avoid the police, and also to avoid aggression and suspicion from other male dealers.

'It's a Man's World'? DJ-ing in Club Spaces

Although DJs and promoters are not criminal occupations in comparison to drug dealing these occupations are located on the margins and firmly embedded in the world of the city at night. It has also been noted (Lovatt 1996) that during the urban regeneration of Manchester those involved in the cultural industries on the margins demanded to be heard and to have a place in this renewal of urban space. 'Clubbing' has become responsible for a number of business offshoots or cultural industries such as music, fashion, club décor, lighting and club promoting. Therefore an analysis of the gendered nature of the production of club spaces and the experiences of women involved as producers of these spaces is important. Two female DJs and promoters, 'Mary' and 'Tina', and a male promoter 'John', were interviewed about their involvement on club scenes as producers of club spaces. These experiences are used to highlight the importance of DJs and promoters on club scenes, and in particular the importance of gendered experiences within these 'professions' are explored.

As the lack of female DJs within club cultures has been well-documented (McRobbie 1994, Milestone and Richards 1999) and this echoes the lack of women within all areas of production associated with club scenes, it is significant that when women do perform a DJ function on the scene, their experience is embedded in the gender expectations formed in other areas of life. One of the most important points to note about club cultures in relation to gender is that the commercialization of club scenes reproduces gender inequalities (Richards and Kruger 1998). The performance of femininities and sexualities are therefore significant for female DJs just as they are for female clubbers who participate in the consumption of these spaces. The two women DJs ('Mary' and 'Tina') clearly had vastly differing experiences in terms of sexism and detrimental male attitudes, and this could be explained in several ways. Firstly 'Tina' had a female DJ and business partner that she played with, thus avoiding difficult contacts with other male DJs. In this sense 'Tina' was not as isolated as 'Mary' and had support and a sense of solidarity with her business partner. Secondly, is the sense of 'Tina's' naïvety which she herself expresses in not always noticing bad male attitudes. In retrospect she acknowledges the double standard in DJ-ing and realizes that, at the time, the sexism 'went over' her head.

> Maybe I'm a bit naïve to it all you know, I think maybe I let a lot of things go over my head and maybe that's why I carry on doing things in lots of male-dominated atmospheres.
>
> (Tina)

Thirdly, it could be a question of sexuality and male attitudes towards differing female sexualities. 'Tina' herself acknowledges that she is very 'boy like' and so was her DJ-ing partner.

We're both very small women, we both look young for our age, and if I'm 30 now I was a little 22 or something then! So I looked really young and I looked like a boy. I think it was to get away from that whole sexy girl image in the club, to try and do something a bit more practical and serious. You didn't want to be there in your little bits showing off all your body like all the other girls were.

(Tina)

'Mary' on the other hand is very feminine in looks, and it could be argued, her looks went against her since although she was good at what she did, she was resented more for it because of her feminine appearance. Therefore it could be partly their contrasting femininities that affected their contrasting experiences of male attitudes in the DJ-ing world. Although 'Tina' feels that men were not trying to be deliberately intimidating:

That whole thing of men standing around the DJ box is really intimidating and that can be taken as they're trying to intimidate you or trying to be rude, but I don't think it is. See, women will come running up going 'oh it's great', but a man won't do that and on the whole they will stand there and nod and that's them showing respect.

(Tina)

Whereas 'Mary's' experiences had been more unpleasant:

When I was first getting gigs he'd be a nightmare with me, he really had it in for me for years and he couldn't stand it that I was a woman and I was alright, he hated it. I had moments when it bothered me but I just ended up getting tough very quickly, but no one will ever get me off the decks now after playing with him, I should shake his hand really for doing me a favour!

(Mary)

The female DJs interviewed have been involved in club scenes for a number of years and have or had a high profile and a good reputation within the club spaces that they helped to produce. One of the questions explored was *why* was there a lack of female DJs and although both women had had unpleasant experiences and felt their gender keenly as DJs, they found it extremely difficult to explain why more women were not attracted to DJ-ing as a profession. 'Mary' expresses herself on the comparatively few numbers of female DJs, and states that she got into DJ-ing by

I just used to blag my way onto the decks at six in the morning when nobody else wanted to do it, when there were thousands of people still there all off their faces. I couldn't mix at all, I was totally rubbish! But just getting up there, there weren't any women doing it really.

(Mary)

'Tina' similarly drifts into DJ-ing through a love of music and playing at informal parties for friends, and is more forthcoming about why it is seen as a male enclave.

I think for me it was love of music, because I was collecting records before I wanted to be a DJ, and your friends know you've got a few good records and doing house parties. I can't really remember what the switch over was; people just asked me eventually 'will you do my club night' and it just grew from that. I think it's that male mentality, that kind of collecting thing. Although music is quite emotional it's quite detached, kind of unemotional, which men are really into and categorizing and having an ego. I am really technically minded, often in a club when you're setting up and putting the plugs in and setting the decks up and everything, people would be surprised that I could do that because I was a girl and I'd often fix things that the blokes couldn't fix and they didn't really like it! I don't think it's a rebellious thing or trying to make a statement, but it is that whole kind of practical mathy collectory man stuff.

(Tina)

Relationships with Customers

In discussing women DJs the gender of the producer is seen to make a difference for those who consume the club night(s). Women DJs had positive relationships with their customers and felt that women in the audience supported them more because they were female. In exploring the experiences of women producers it is apparent they felt that they attended to the needs of their consumers more than their male equivalents. It is this nurturing of and attention to needs that women DJs felt that they brought to their performance for consumers of club spaces:

I would say most female DJs care a bit more, I've seen a couple of famous ones who don't give a shit, but I'd say in general women do care a bit more. I definitely play for women naturally, I don't mean to but women generally like my music, so I've always had a lot of support off them.

(Mary)

Both participants stated that they got a positive response from women and felt that female DJs were more 'in touch' with how the crowd was responding, and that they could 'read' the crowd better.

I think they tend to play more music that just gets you and I think that women are more emotionally in touch than men and I think the music reflects that. Blokes tend to play a lot more beats beats beats on top and it's a heavy kind of aggressive thing and women tend to play more vocally emotionally more uplifting stuff.

(Tina)

Crowd responses towards female DJs were seen to be different depending on what type of club the women were working in. Different groups of women were also seen to have varying tastes regarding the music they preferred to hear and this supports the view that music is important to female clubbers. For example, lesbian women were seen by 'Tina' to have different music tastes to straight women.

I would think about the music they wanted to hear but more because they were gay not because they were women, so I'd take a bit more housey uplifting stuff. Maybe that's giving women a bit of credit that I don't need to do anything special for them, I'm catering for them as people not women, or that women have never been catered for so you just don't think about it, and they only get catered to for being lesbians because they're a sexuality group.

(Tina)

Lesbian women were seen to react differently to DJs in general but because of issues relating to sexuality not just gender.

It's wicked! It's brilliant 'cos girls know how to have fun, especially lesbian girls who might feel more put down and repressed, so they can go out and let loose and have fun; its great to be in a club with just women.

(Tina)

An imbalance within club scenes was identified from the experiences of women DJs, and a feeling that more women were needed to influence these spaces to make them better and more diverse. There was also a sense of anger at women DJs who tried to emulate men and did not put their heart and soul into pleasing the crowd although it was recognized that they are expected to fit in with established conventions and ways of working. As in most areas of work, women DJs have to adopt the strategy of 'blending in' to the existing organizational culture. Women within the music industry spoke of the way that management and key decision-making jobs were dominated by an 'old boy network' from which women were excluded (Negus 1992). There was a consensus between the two female DJs that women should not try and 'be one of the boys', which excluded them from this 'old boy network', but be true to themselves and DJ in their own style.

I've known women DJs and they kind of end up like the blokes instead of doing it like a woman they do it like the men do and that annoys me. I think you should stand by being a woman, you owe it to women really. Women should do it their own way because I think the scene needs a woman's influence, there's imbalance still. If I was doing a club and nobody was dancing I'd be gutted, but I'd just have to work harder. I want to fill that floor and have everybody going home saying it was the best night in ages.

(Mary)

Producers and consumers of differing club scenes are seen as cultural intermediaries and they have an important role in the transmission of new style (Featherstone 1990). This is especially relevant in the case of DJs and promoters who are the gatekeepers of the 'cutting edge' as the development of new consumption and leisure spaces such as clubs precipitate the transmission of new styles. However, it is questionable whether the old cultural hierarchies such as high/low/elite/popular/mass/minority are becoming redundant as these categories still exist in the micro sense *within* new cultural spaces such as clubs. There are still underlying inequalities such as the feminization of bad taste, DJ snobbery and designer fashion associated with clubbing.

Female DJs as the Excluded 'Other'

One of the reasons why more women are not attracted to DJ-ing are the poor attitudes towards women by established male DJs. However the attitudes of male DJs varied in different spaces and bad attitudes towards female DJs seemed to relate to the size of the crowd being played to or to the popularity and 'hipness' of the club concerned. Therefore by playing in a club space that is seen as 'hip' the DJ accumulates 'subcultural capital' (Thornton 1995), and some male DJs resented 'Tina' and 'Mary' for accumulating this 'subcultural capital', by playing well. While attitudes towards female consumers are perceived to be more equal in *undergrounds*, this is not necessarily the case for female producers within the same spaces. The more 'hip' the venue, and the larger the potential for accumulating 'subcultural capital', the more difficult DJ-ing becomes. One of the barriers encountered in relation to the attitudes of some male DJs are mentioned in the quote below, in discussing a large illegal 'rave' some years before, when 'Mary' first started DJ-ing:

> When I first started in (names club night), the male DJs had a serious attitude, it was a proper battle up there, there was 10,000 people to play to which is major (in terms of kudos) and everyone wanted that position.
>
> (Mary)

A number of other problems and stresses were identified as coming with the job such as nerves, and the responsibility of having the making or breaking of a good night in their hands, and these were also cited as reasons why women would not want to be involved in the production of club spaces. Also other DJs not being supportive or having a problem with her as a woman were cited as making life difficult by 'Mary'.

> Some other DJs for whatever reason, maybe they're jealous, maybe they think they should have an attitude, they could make your life hell. I'm picking out the negative side really 'cos there's lots who don't care if you're a woman or not. Others have really bad attitudes and wait for your mistakes, and I feel you have to be double good if you're a woman because they will slag you off, they don't treat you any easier, they treat you worse in a way.
>
> (Mary)

'Tina' finds that one of the problems for her was the 'herding' of women DJs together, which could be a positive experience, but she felt it was equivalent to saying they could not compete with male DJs in the 'real' world, and were just booked for 'women's' nights.

I've been interviewed about women's things like they'd get six or seven women together and ask us questions and very often we'd be pulled together for a women's night and a promoter would put on a women's night and try and get all the women DJs together and it would be like again, can't we just be hired because you like what we do!

(Tina)

Interestingly, even though 'Tina' states that she had no overt problems with sexist attitudes, there is an underlying tone that although she did get 'respect' for what she did there was a 'double pressure' on her to be good.

I never did, actually I just found that I got more respect for what I was doing because I was a woman and it was good like that and no one was ever mean or rude or anything. I think the chance was there because at first they would be quite sceptical and you'd be feeling like you were really being watched and judged but I felt like I lived up to it and because I lived up to it then they liked me even more. It was like a double pressure, which is why at first I was so *so* scared.

(Tina)

'Tina' and 'Mary' highlight that the expectations of female DJs are much lower than for their male counterparts.[4] They are not expected to be technically as proficient, but 'get away' with not mixing[5] for example because they are women. However, if you were a woman others were more impressed if you were technically proficient because it was not expected.

People expect if you're going to be a proper DJ you should be able to mix, but you do meet a lot of women DJs who don't mix and they get away with that. I remember my first night DJ-ing a real proper club, I did know I could do it because I could mix well. Blokes don't expect you to be able to or people in general didn't expect you to be able to, 'cos a lot of girls get away with not mixing when really you do need to, and in the same way they do get away with it because they are girls and people give them a bit more, but then if you can do that side of things they're even more impressed.

(Tina)

While it has been suggested that the position of women in the music industry has been improving (Negus 1992) the experiences of 'Tina' and 'Mary' do not seem to bear that out. Some male DJs harass their female equivalents, which takes a lot of determination to ignore. It can be argued that women are just not taken seriously by some men and so they have to work twice as hard to gain recognition. Women are also marginalized in discussions of popular culture and gender it seems simply does not mesh with the masculine creation that is 'rock', whose ideals have dominated the production industries (Negus 1992). Therefore

---

4   Due to the lack of data on the subject of female producers, with the notable exception of Milestone and Richards (1999), the observations made are based on the interviews conducted both with the producers themselves, and the wider research sample.

5   Mixing refers to the technical processes involved in blending tracks together to create a seamless change over from one to the other.

the dominant discourse that infuses the cultural production industries is that of a male dominated, outdated, rock-based ideal. In keeping with this outdated, rock ideal, 'Mary' states that some male egos cannot cope with the fact that she is a woman and proficient at what she does.

> Or they give you more shit if you play good and you're a woman because they can't handle it, it's an ego thing! And that just does their heads in especially if you're better than them. It makes me play better really, I wouldn't have got this far if I weren't strong, I would have been wiped out by now, plenty of women are. It's not the easiest job for a woman.
>
> (Mary)

Involvement in the cultural industries as consumers or for work includes participation in urban spaces, which raises issues of gendered use of the city. There are limitations to women's participation in the night time economy of the cultural industries and a study found that only twenty nine per cent of users of Manchester city centre after six thirty in the evening were female (Taylor et al. 1996). Networking within these industries is often an area where women feel excluded as it tends to take place in bars and clubs at night. Fears for personal safety, domestic responsibilities as well as fears of appearing sexually available inhibit women's individual participation. Thus similar constraints operate on women who are involved in the production of club spaces that operate on women who are the consumers of club spaces.

There were contradictions about the sexism and bad attitudes from male DJs in some of the responses from 'Tina' and 'Mary'. It is these contradictions which are interesting in themselves as they highlight the complex and problematic nature of gendered relations in the night time economy of club spaces, within professions such as DJ-ing. Women DJs are discriminated against at differing levels, but are reluctant to actually state it is discrimination that is the problem, as this was something that they did not always recognize at the time it occurred. With experience it became apparent that discrimination on the grounds of gender explained certain behaviour and this is summed up when talking about the denial of sexist behaviour that in hindsight was very obvious:

> The thing I really feel from being a woman is that, I never admitted for years me that it was a sexist thing, but other female DJs did. It's dawned on me in the last couple of years that it was affecting me. There's certain promoters in this city that have not supported me and I could play as well as any of their DJs, so I've had to work five times as hard and do it for myself.
>
> (Mary)

However being excluded from certain groups may not be an issue that is solely related to gender as 'Mary' states that belonging or inclusion also comes with being part of the cliques which run club spaces. Although these powerful cliques are also made up of predominantly male members making gender a factor that affects membership of these groups.

The thing is not so much being a woman, but I'm not very good at being in a little DJ clique, and that really stalls me. Most of my mates are not in the music industry, I prefer it that way as if I ever got on a pretentious one me mates would be the first to say 'who the fuck do you think you are?!', and if you're in that clique you've got nothing to reflect off, people tell you you're great all the time, and it all becomes really fickle. I think that's halted me more than being a woman.

(Mary)

The discrimination against women DJs is commented on by Logan (1998), in his critique of *Ministry* magazine[6] in an article entitled 'So you want to be a DJ? Let's see your legs' (Brian Logan July 1998, The *Guardian*, 4). *Ministry* magazine is positioned as being guilty of promoting women DJs in terms of their sexuality rather than in terms of how good they are at what they do.

Therefore as for 'Melanie' in negotiating the male world of drug dealing, the male world of DJ-ing is also problematic for 'Tina' and 'Mary' and there are similarities that can be drawn out between their experiences. DJ-ing also involved risk and uncertainty from a financial and professional viewpoint; the 'making' or 'breaking' of a club night. A certain amount of self-esteem and confidence was needed to 'face down' any male harassment, particularly in 'Mary's' case where she was on her own. The 'macho' environment of DJ-ing has parallels with the 'macho', male world of dealing that are difficult to negotiate, as women are excluded from the inner cliques and powerful positions in both areas.

Club Promoting – A Man's World?

Promoting club spaces can be seen as a distinct category separate from, but linked to, production and marketing. Both 'Mary' and 'Tina', DJs at and promoters of club nights argue that the main factor in assuring success is the groundwork involved in promoting an event; distribution of flyers, negotiation of space, ensuring that the 'scene is set', and that the 'right' sorts of consumers will be attracted to specific places.

When (names club) was really big, the big Saturday night in Manchester, very glamorous, very expensive. Because it was a serious business and we were all promoting our own sections we had to meet up every week about the promotion of the club. Dealing with publicity and trying to get write ups and stuff like that is similar to the extent that you have to step into the same kind of world of boy talk and 'bigging' yourself up, but it's a different vibe.

(Tina)

Both 'Tina' and 'Mary' were involved in either promoting themselves as DJs, their own club nights or the clubs they worked in. 'Mary' as well as DJ-ing, promotes a club night on what could be termed a 'casual' basis, in the way that

---

6   'Ministry' is one of the main dance magazines relating to all aspects of clubbing.

it is not a regular occurrence, and tends to be a 'one off' every couple of months. This is seen to be the most effective and creative way to promote clubs, as the promoters are DJs and close to the crowd. Therefore the producers of club scenes are 'barely distinguishable from the consumers' (Haslam 1999, 217). This is true of the smaller underground club spaces, but there is a difference in the larger more mainstream clubs, where the producers of club spaces are more removed from the consumers of those same spaces. The challenge or problematic issue is how to explain *why* it is the case that DJ-ing and promoting are male dominated professions. For the female DJs and promoters represented here although it was an accepted fact that they were few in number, exploring 'why' proved to be extremely difficult, again highlighting the complex nature of gendered relationships in this sphere.

> It's just that male state of mind of collecting, showing off things like that. From a DJs point of view that's what it starts off as, men are naturally drawn to that and women aren't and I think that's why you don't get very many women collecting records they're just not into it from a natural point of view. From a promoting point of view I'm not really sure, you'd think there would be a lot more women promoters because its just about gob, confidence and a lot of women are good at that just chatting and bigging things up so I don't know why there's not so many women promoters, but then it comes down to it you're going to step into a man's world and maybe they don't want to do it 'cos its intimidating that's probably why, its easy to stay away from.
>
> (Tina)

One explanation that is implicit in 'Mary' and 'Tina's' accounts is that a form of hegemonic masculinity is at work in the world of DJ-ing and promoting. Although these professions do not involve breaking the law they are ruled by similar hierarchical attitudes and sets of rules as drug dealing is and women are again positioned as the intrusive 'other'. Male DJs tend to avoid discussing labels and producers with 'fans' or clubbers, avoiding the dissipation of power. Therefore the worlds of club DJs and promoters are characterized by shared knowledge and as is the case with female drug dealers, female DJs are not included in this sharing of knowledge. Male DJs are not prepared to give away any of their 'subcultural capital' to their female counterparts. Thus ensuring they remain powerful and this underlines these professions as male dominated and effectively blocks women from these social groupings. 'Mary' suggests that she has not been promoted as much as she could have been, as she does not socialize with other DJs, particularly those she sees as pretentious. Therefore the exclusion of women DJs and promoters and the difficulties in belonging to a male dominated culture for women are apparent all the time, not just in the acts of DJ-ing or the processes of promoting. The intimidation experienced by stepping into a male dominated world such as promoting was one of the reasons why women were discouraged from entering the industry. 'Mary' and 'Tina' felt that negotiating this hegemonic masculine culture was like a battle, with meetings being talked about in terms of 'holding your ground'.

Dominated by men, by egos, it's that whole thing of male music industry, it's drugs sex and ego which men love. You're trying to get respect for what you're doing, so it was very much that male atmosphere. It was like holding your ground a lot in the meetings which I found intimidating. We'd all sit round a table, it was a big boys club and we did have to make an effort to be seen and say something, to be together and to be not drippy about things, not like two little girls running their room and be in control.

(Tina)

Women promoters were also seen to have to try harder in the same way as women who were DJs. There were lower expectations on women involved in promoting, but also the same 'double pressure' faced by female DJs of having to work twice as hard to gain respect.

When you're in a really male atmosphere, if men are given a reason to respect you I've always found the men do give you the respect and they do take you in so, I never felt uncomfortable like that. In some ways they give you more of a chance, I suppose in a way they expect less from you, it's that same thing when you're DJ-ing, people come up and they're surprised. They hang around because they didn't expect it in the first place, so if you do live up to their expectations they give you double respect.

(Tina)

It was highlighted that as well as being scrutinized more closely women promoters and DJs had to be better to even get a break in the first place.

You don't even get the chance to be good or crap if you're a woman you've got to be really good to get there in the first place. But if you are good I've always felt that because I have been good, they're watching you double close at the beginning but as long as you pass you get respect.

(Tina)

When questioned about the problems of promoting a club night practical concerns tended to be the main issues: publicity, DJs, venue, and the fact that it is very stressful to organize everything and get it right. In fact 'Mary' stated that she got PPT (pre-promoting tension) instead of PMT (pre-menstrual tension)!

It's the most stressful job in the music business definitely. You've got to be very un-personal about it which I find a bit difficult. You're thinking about the DJs, the lights, the smoke machine, the door – have you made enough money? Are there enough punters in? You've got all the blaggers on the door, leading up to that you've got to flyer all the clubs till three in the morning. It's a good feeling though when the clubs full and it does well and everybody has a good time, it's very satisfying.

(Mary)

Just having a failure really just having a night that doesn't work or if you're DJ-ing and you really fuck up, you can do a few terrible mixes it's a horrible feeling and you can clear a dance floor ... and I have done all of those things!!

(Tina)

The pressures on women involved in club promoting and DJ-ing were numerous but one of the risks most commonly identified was a 'shame' risk, as other promoters would be checking to see if different nights were going well.

> It's a shame risk because it's really shameful to run a flop! You check out all your competition and everyone will doing that so you'd always see on a Saturday night everyone would be popping in to everyone else's night to see whose getting who in.
>
> (Tina)

And another problem was finance:

> Losing money, I've lost thousands, lost four hundred pounds at the last one which is nothing if you talk to some promoters, see (names person) is a good promoter because he doesn't take it personally, it's like gambling, you win some, you lose some, you can do everything perfect, the formula can be right and it can be dead.
>
> (Mary)

> Spent all that money and told all your mates and nobody comes down, except your mates and they're standing there on their own, and the club is empty, and you've lost a load of money. You just feel a bit stupid like having a birthday party and nobody turns up!
>
> (Tina)

So, illustrations of why promoting in particular has not attracted more women, may be the irregular hours, stress, having to be out until the early hours of the morning on a consistent basis and the financial losses, coupled with the negotiation of an hegemonic masculine culture. The same sexual division of labour exists within the cultural industries as it does in more conventional types of work and employment. Although within the cultural industries working practices and organizational culture can be both supportive and detrimental to the women involved (Milestone and Richards 1999). The music and cultural industries are frequently cited as being flexible, creative and innovative with the dividing line between work and leisure being blurred, but this 'flexibility' can also be seen as a constraint, as workers need to be able to blur work and leisure. This blurring of work and leisure has consequences for women who are parents and for DJs having to do 'tours', work late hours precludes parenthood or makes it very difficult. As 'Tina' states:

> Because I chose to have children, that was the end of it really when I got pregnant. I decided to give it up, because I couldn't possibly do both at the same time.
>
> (Tina)

However, some women preferred this 'flexibility' as it allowed them to mix their roles and work outside a nine to five pattern. On the one hand 'flexibility' meant working long hard anti-social hours such as ninety hour weeks, but on the other hand women interpreted 'flexibility' in a positive light as something which enabled them to work and fulfil other domestic roles (Milestone and Richards 1999). 'Tina' emphasizes these long anti-social hours:

It takes a lot of hard work to do promoting I was never a very good promoter; none of my nights were really successful. I was doing it as a DJ promoting, which is a bit weak, most good promoters are just promoters. You have to live that life you're checking out all the other clubs all the time, you're on the phone constantly, you're just on it all the time and to me it's quite boring.

(Tina)

However in these terms it's a wonder anyone is a promoter, but perhaps the irregularity of it as a profession puts women in particular off. 'Mary' was a DJ first and a promoter second, so she was not constantly facing the promoting stresses such as availability of venues.

I've never really had a problem finding them (venues for club nights) really, I mean it's hard to get a regular thing on a weekend, but if you want 'one offs', see I'm not like other promoters, it's not the main thing that I do so if I couldn't get a venue, I'd wait until the next month.

(Mary)

A focal issue for women DJs and promoters is how male colleagues reacted to them and whether this affected their work, or how seriously they were taken in the promoting world. Despite the problems faced by being a woman in a male dominated business, there was a feeling that even if male attitudes left a lot to be desired, if you could get someone to listen to you as a woman you were given more of a chance because it was so unusual for women to be in these kinds of business. Although this optimistic view needs to be taken in conjunction with previous statements about working harder to get a 'foot in the door' and the 'double pressure' to excel.

There was a bit more of all that 'hey babe' stuff, bit more like that, but they would be interested in you because you are a woman and because you're doing something good, it's almost like they would listen more intently and be a bit more 'really, right'. I always enjoyed it as a positive being part of a male dominated thing, it felt like more of an achievement.

(Tina)

One of the other main problems for promoters, and this does not just relate to female promoters, is the prevalence of drug use at their nights, although their attitudes towards use of drugs were fairly casual as the following quote shows.

I try and go for venues where they will let you skin up in peace, because I think you should let people do that. But I do believe that my punters should be decent enough to hide and not be blatant. I'm a great believer in if people are keeping it down then the club can't get into trouble unless its obvious, I think people should be a bit careful and respect the club. As far as other drugs are concerned, probably my nights are people on pills, and if anyone asks me I never know anyway, I just let people get on with it.

(Mary)

Promoters also had their share of problems associated with gang trouble at nights they had put on, resulting in the closing down of these nights by choice to avoid any further instances.

> I've had nights where trouble has come to it but we've not set out to attract that kind of audience. We used to do a drum and bass night, but it turned a little bit nasty and when that started happening we pulled it.
>
>   (John)

It was a downside for promoters not only in the obvious sense of having to cope with aggression, bad attitudes and violence, but because it disrupted an audience that they had nurtured over a period of time, who mixed well and made a good night. An element causing friction puts an end to months of hard work, although 'John' highlights that clubbers are generally not interested in starting trouble and tend not to 'play up' to anyone who is, which means that any trouble is dissipated before it begins.

> The stuff that I'm involved in now it's very rare you get an appearance from anybody there to cause trouble. Sometimes they can't cope and leave 'cos nobody shows them any respect and everyone's just having a good time and they leave. It goes right over their heads and I like that to have that effect on them, it does their heads in.
>
>   (John)

It is also ironic that the use of ecstasy a drug which increases empathy towards others and a sense of being 'luved up' has precipitated the rise in violence in some club spaces.

> Another key factor in the upsurge in violence in Manchester's club land was the way fuel for club goers underwent a huge change from alcohol to ecstasy. This created markets for drugs in and around clubs, and a battle for control of those markets ensued.
>
>   (Haslam 1999, 196)

Therefore perhaps the fragmentation of club spaces, particularly the core of small friendly club spaces reduces the risk of violence. The money involved from the door takings or drug use within these smaller spaces is not enough to tempt organized crime to take over. The larger more mainstream or corporate clubs with big crowd capacities that make a lot more money and have larger drug markets become victims of their own success and attract unwanted attention.

The experiences of women involved in the production of club scenes, demonstrates that for women to enter male dominated 'professions' is an uphill battle. The uncertainty and riskiness of promoting a night that may fail through no fault of their own was one issue that made promoting difficult, although this does not just apply to women in this field. But, as with dealing and DJ-ing, a certain amount of male prejudice needed to be overcome to be taken seriously within the area of club promoting. For women in these professions, the lines of exclusion and power are drawn in spaces that they may not have access to (Straw 1996), so that in a sense women are always on the 'outside looking in'.

This chapter has identified and analysed the performance of gender played out in the production of club spaces. The arguments raised highlight that female producers of club spaces are disadvantaged in many ways because of their gender. I now turn to an examination of the experiences of female clubbers to explore the relationship of their gendered positions to the consumption of club spaces while using drugs and taking 'risks'.

Chapter 4

Pleasure and Risk: Drug Use and Club Scenes[1]

Introduction

In this chapter discussions about risk and pleasure are developed to explore how women experience the use of substances such as ecstasy, amphetamine and cocaine within club scenes. Society has difficulty categorizing women who use drugs recreationally because they are an 'in between' category. There is only language for describing female drug users as bad both in the criminological sense and in the feminine sense, they are seen as 'doubly deviant' (Gelsthorpe 1989). Trying to fit female clubbers who are recreational drug users into this category does not give an adequate insight into their behaviour nor their challenges to this narrow stereotypical bad girl image. In adolescence, which is a masculine concept (Lees 1993), girls cannot behave like typical adolescents, moodily recklessly and rebelliously without infringing upon the dictates of femininity. The double standard acts as a set of controls upon girls sexualities. However, as women move beyond their teenage years feminism and challenges to the 'double standard' become more popular (Lees 1993). So, how do female clubbers in their twenties and thirties challenge the double standard and their 'double deviant' status, and how do these controls and constraints affect their reading and construction of their own sexualities?

In the contemporary society of the 1990s and 2000s there has been a widening of lifestyle choices for young women which produces tension between a feminine identity shaped by forces such as feminism and more conventional modes of femininity (Budgeon in Innes 1998). What is lacking in discussions about female drug users and clubbers is the acknowledgement that women are competent social actors that produce their own identities. This is not to deny that structural constraints operate on young women to limit them but the *reaction* of young women to these constrains needs careful consideration. The clubbing women discussed in this chapter recognized the 'double standard' and the constraints that operated upon them, and they deconstructed these with varying degrees of success when they encountered them. Female clubbers negotiate their identities in a social world that has increased possibilities and opportunities, but also contains increased risk and uncertainty (Giddens 1991). So how do female

---

1   The use of the terms 'scenes' relates to describing both underground and mainstream clubs collectively. The term 'space' usually refers to a particular type of club(s) or 'space(s)'.

clubbers negotiate these contradictory social conditions whilst also challenging the double standard? It is important to consider how far in the liberated late 20th and early 21st centuries is there an ambiguous response to girls who are 'up for it'.

Women Clubbers and Drugs

How women plan and view their own drug use in the context of their participation in club scenes is important as media panics about clubbing lifestyles represent young women as victims of unscrupulous drug dealers, and as being passive and uneducated about the use of drugs.

> Where a guy takes a helpless young girl back to his flat to rape her; where a young girl wakes up in bed with a 'mysterious attractive stranger' and can't remember what she has done because she has taken ecstasy; where a dealer sells rubbish to strangers.

> (Williamson 1997, 55)

Women clubbers contradicted this stereotypical view of passive, uneducated 'victims' as they were careful about their drug use; buying drugs from trusted people, and planning evenings with drugs involving a whole social package of going out. Although, some female clubbers stated that while they were not always organized in planning their evenings out, they still tried to minimize risk when using drugs. The use of ecstasy was seen as enhancing an evening out in terms of relating to the music and the atmosphere, but not necessarily as an essential ingredient. Drugs were taken because it was fun and pleasurable to do so, not because of any malign pressure from others. As 'Ruth' described her night out:

> Starts off with alcohol and food to get into the swing, having something to eat together, drinking and then speed or coke, you're unlikely to do a pill until you're in a club, it's all planned and quite careful. Smoking draw at the end of the evening to help people chill out and come down, maybe drink again.

> (Ruth)

Female clubber's definitions of recreational drug use are also important as recreational drug use by women is under-researched and under-theorized. Investigating whether women clubbers attached any meaning to the phrase 'recreational drug use' and how they identified their own drug taking within these definitions is important. The comments made by female clubbers demonstrated that the phrase had meaning for them relating to pleasure and socializing. It was also evident from the way female clubbers described the term 'recreational drug use' that it was very much seen in *opposition* to problematic drug addiction such as injecting heroin use. Therefore women who are recreational drug users define their behaviour in specific ways. According to 'Alice':

I'd say taking drugs to enjoy yourself when you're out in a club or for the evening and it's something that's not abused day in day out, it's more a choice factor rather than anything you would have to do if it was a habit.

(Alice)

'Ruth' defined the phrase as 'Drug use that fits into your life, rather than your life fitting into your drug use.' Therefore recreational drug use for these women was an activity that was based around fun, pleasure and socialising, rather than the stereotypical images of addiction and abuse. It was important for women clubbers to be in control of their drug use as it was only a fun part of their lives. For some female clubbers other responsibilities such as children or work were more central than drug use, as 'Ruth' outlines: 'Clubbing is a good part of my life, but with my career and kids it can't take over as they are central now.'

Women clubbers defined the term 'recreational drug use' as a pattern of drug use that does not interfere with other areas of life and work and most felt that their drug use fitted this pattern. Women who are recreational drug users have normal jobs, lives, relationships, ambitions and aspirations and this challenges the stereotypes and assumptions made about women who use drugs, that they are polluted, diseased and bad. Other studies of recreational drug use have found that young women were more than happy to talk about their drug use, in the context of recreational leisure use. They were able to maintain a wide range of life options beyond their drug use, with some being involved in low level dealing (Henderson 1996). A good proportion of the female clubbers who participated in the research which underpins this book had responsible professional jobs, and four were single parents. Recreational drug use for these women did not affect their day-to-day responsibilities. However, a small proportion of female clubbers said that they felt their drug use had crossed over the line from being recreational to being problematic, although they recognized this and stopped using drugs altogether for a while. According to 'Evelyn':

I think it did probably cross that line towards the end. When I went through a bad patch and felt really low I definitely used it to escape, as a way to forget about things, to feel happy for a few hours, and it stopped being fun, and that's when I stopped shortly afterwards.

(Evelyn)

'Diane' described her experience:

Where I was living in (names country) because they have got such a blasé attitude towards drugs and you get a bit carried away in that environment, I don't think it would have happened to me if I wasn't there.

(Diane)

The fact that clubbers do not just use ecstasy but are polydrug users is a common research finding (Meesham et al. 2000; Hunt and Evans 2003; Kilfoyle and Bellis 1998) and it is recognized that some clubbers also use drugs that are more often used by those who are problematic, addicted drug users (Hunt and Evans 2003). The female clubbers who stated that their drug use became a problem were more likely to use a variety of drugs in various mixtures to produce better or different states of being high, such as ecstasy and acid, ecstasy and amphetamines or cocaine. Also because clubbing is based around the use of stimulants such as ecstasy and amphetamines the use of depressants such as heroin to 'comedown' from the intense high of club drugs was highlighted by female clubbers. Other prescription drugs such as 'Valium' were also noted by female clubbers to aid in the 'comedown' [2] process and to help them sleep. In addition alcohol was commonly used for this reason, to aid in 'coming down' and to help clubbers get to sleep. The use of 'Temazepan' by Scottish clubbers (Hunt and Evans 2003) is likely to have been used for similar reasons, to aid in the 'comedown' process. It is apparent therefore that female clubbers use a variety of drugs including substances that have traditionally been defined as problematic. This highlights further that recreational drug use by clubbing women needs to be explored in a different way as those who use drugs in this way cannot be accounted for in official discourses about female drug use (Ettorre 1992).

Attitudes to Women who do Drugs

Historically young women using drugs in a recreational manner have been viewed in terms of contamination, control and 'ruin' of the women involved (Khon 1992). In contemporary social spaces such as clubs it is still the case that women who use drugs are a target for some men to harass or be sexually threatening towards. Female clubbers highlighted that there were still stereotypical images of women who take drugs, but also that male attitudes towards drug-using women were different within club spaces from that of male 'outsiders'. The extent to which drug usage on club scenes is empowering for female clubbers or reflects their subordination depends upon attitudes to the 'other' in differing club spaces. In the spaces of *mainstreams* and *undergrounds*, attitudes towards women using drugs will not be the same. These differences relate to ideas and attitudes towards sexuality within these spaces and to the visibility of women within these different scenes, *because* of their sexuality. Female clubbers were more visible in spaces where they were expected to conform to traditional ways of expressing femininities that emphasized them as sexual objects and sexualized them through constraints on style. Not all club spaces are the same in this respect so women's experiences depend on where they are and who else is present and overall underground clubs were felt to be more empowering for women than mainstream spaces. Mainstream spaces because of their heightened emphasis on sexuality led to less empowerment through drug usage. Female clubbers stated that that some men would see women who had taken ecstasy as being more 'up for it' sexually, and that this put pressure on them to have casual sex or be sexually expressive. 'Ruth' felt that:

---

2   The comedown period refers to a day or two days after drugs such as ecstasy have been taken. Clubbers commonly state that they feel tired and/or anxious and more emotionally fragile or vulnerable in this stage. Another issue associated with the 'comedown' is the purity of the drug. The purer the drug, the less pronounced the effects of the 'comedown'.

The idea is that a woman has taken ecstasy so she will be a lot more expressive and some men will play on that. There is the feeling that because she's trashed, some kind of crap behaviour is acceptable.

(Ruth)

Drug-using women are still constructed as 'fallen' or contaminated and the double standard inherent in wider society also operates on club spaces and acts to constrain female clubbers who use drugs. Therefore this is a risk that women in contemporary society take in choosing to behave in this way, as by using drugs they are risking others viewing them as 'loose' and treating them accordingly. However it was highlighted that the types of men who would harass women would do so whatever the situation. It would not matter which kind of spaces they were in or what substances they were using, their *attitude* meant that their behaviour was unwelcome in all clubbing situations. As 'Naomi' stated, in describing male behaviour:

If they're gonna hassle you, they're gonna hassle you. I don't think it makes any difference to them. They might prefer you to be on drugs 'cos you might be less aggressive towards them, some fluffy 'I've had a pill and everyone's my mate' chick.

(Naomi)

Participating on club scenes is not all 'one happy experience' for women, but with the explosion in club scenes that 'rave' precipitated, clubbing women are more visible in public not only in the clubs themselves, but also in traversing the city at night through the pursuit of leisure. Female clubbers are publicly pleasure seeking, using illegal drugs and are therefore also much more visible to police and law enforcement agencies than in previous decades. An interesting question when exploring stereotypes of women who use drugs is whether the emergence of female drug use in the public sphere in club spaces had any effect on the development of negative social attitudes towards female recreational drug users. Perceived parental attitudes towards drug-using women were explored as examples of social attitudes towards female recreational drug users and to illustrate how those outside club spaces viewed women who used drugs. Some responses in relation to parental attitudes were unexpected, as 'Linda' said of her male parent:

My dad has taken more drugs than I have, including the amounts and the types. My mother is totally anti-drugs, but I know when she was younger she did speed and smoked weed. My dad is very clued up and he just wants to know where you got it from, in case anything happens, so he knows who's doing what dodgy, he's got quite a few connections.

(Linda)

The main parental reactions were perceived to be worry and disapproval if they knew that their daughters were taking illegal drugs such as ecstasy partly because of the media panics surrounding club scenes. These parental reactions were also associated with the perceived risks of taking recreational drugs, which had been highlighted by cases of deaths due to ecstasy use, such as Leah Betts.[3] This highlights that the normalization of drug use is not necessarily apparent in all sections of society. Clubbers themselves may feel that it is 'normal' to use drugs such as ecstasy but this is not necessarily the case with other social groups. Women clubbers take risks with their sexual and physical safety, through the quality of the drugs they take, through breaking the law, and risking the disapproval of 'society', although the personal risk in terms of disappointment of loved ones is not to be underestimated. 'Anne' described her feelings as:

> I confided in my mother once as she was saying 'come on, you have haven't you?', so I confided in her that I'd taken drugs and she went bonkers! So I had to retract it all and say it was one toke on a spliff. They would be terrified if they knew I took drugs as often as I did, and they would think it was incredibly immature and irresponsible.
>
> (Anne)

'Sheila' anticipated her parents' response:

> They could just about cope with the fact that I might have taken cannabis in my time, but they would be horrified if they knew I'd taken more serious drugs. They still have the 'drugs will kill you mentality', and also they're not educated, they're only educated about drugs by the media, which isn't the best education to have.
>
> (Sheila)

Therefore parents' reactions were perceived to be very disapproving towards drug use, and most female clubbers felt they would not share the fact that they took drugs with their parents. There was a concern about the images of drug use that were portrayed in the media and picked upon by parents and those outside club spaces as a true picture. Most women clubbers felt they would like parents and 'outsiders' to be better educated about drug use and to rethink their attitudes towards those who use drugs in a recreational way.

Drug use is approached in different ways in *mainstreams* and *undergrounds*; one is a frenetic, isolating 'do as much as you can' experience, the other is a more friendly, socially-centred experience. Clearly the risk factor associated with drug use is greater in the first environment than the second. The *Attitude* of those attending in terms of drug use and female sexuality affects risk as it structures the meanings surrounding difference in club spaces. *Attitude* becomes important in discussing drug use, as the social rules regarding taking drugs which are found in different spaces, increase or decrease the risk factors for female clubbers. An example of differentiated risk is described by 'Anne' as she recalls an unpleasant night out and describes why the club space in question was unsafe from her point of view:

---

3   Leah Betts was a young woman who died after taking ecstasy in 1995. Her parents gave permission for pictures of her in intensive care in hospital to be used in an anti-drugs campaign.

Really mad, everyone totally trolleyed (in an advanced state of intoxication), and it was horrible, quite hard techno, everywhere you looked there were men pawing over women and I remember being pushed across the dance floor. You just think no, totally unsafe ... places aren't the same ... it's not safe.

(Anne)

Apart from parents, other people outside club scenes were also perceived to be disapproving and critical of women who use drugs, but from a viewpoint of ignorance compounded by fear of the unknown. Outsiders were perceived not to understand how important it was for women to remain in control and female clubbers therefore felt that their drug use and clubbing behaviour was misunderstood. The focus here has been on the 'meanings' that women clubbers attach to their drug use as recreational, and how they feel their behaviour is wrongly judged by those outside club scenes. Drug use is a unifying factor between those who participate in club scenes, and the use of ecstasy especially helps to break down everyday social barriers. Female clubbers and recreational drug users were responsible about their drug use and for a majority of them it was an enjoyable part of their lives that did not interfere with their other responsibilities.

Challenging Stereotypes of Drug-Using Women

Marginalization and stigmatization are two issues that affect drug-using women as women drug users are viewed negatively by society and stereotyped as mad, bad or sexually available (Ettorre 1992; Khon 1992; Rosenbaum 1985). Therefore stereotypical images of women clubbers and recreational drug users will be explored to identify whether these images stand up to close scrutiny. How women account for their drug use was examined with female clubbers and one significant conclusion is that women make an effort to take ecstasy and other drugs in environments where they feel safe. For example, 'Lucy' describes her drug usage as:

Very safe but that was to do with the place I was in and the people I was with. I think that your first experience of taking drugs you need to be very safe. Saying that you generally need to be, I wouldn't be able to take something if I didn't feel comfortable in my surroundings and the people I was with, I don't think that would be wise anyway.

(Lucy)

Women clubbers who are recreational drug users take ecstasy and other club drugs such as amphetamines, whilst being aware of their responsibilities for the effects induced by their consumption of illegal substances and for their own safety.[4] However the use of drugs on club scenes has changed over the years with a trend towards using other drugs such as cocaine, and depressants such as heroin to 'come down' from the big high of ecstasy or amphetamines. This was a concern for female

---

4   It is recognized that not all women will minimize risk when using drugs in a clubbing environment.

clubbers even if they had not taken depressant drugs themselves. 'Sheila' highlights her concern about heroin use and drink-spiking:

> I have no experience of people taking heroin as part of the rave scene, but I've heard that people are doing that which I find really worrying, getting into the realms of non-recreational drug use. I've heard of other stuff linked to the rave scene like Rohypnol[5] which is a nasty date-rape drug, which can be dropped into people's drinks and makes them black out for hours with no memory of what happened.
>
> (Sheila)

And 'Ruth' describes how:

> I've used smack as a coming back from the club and 'coming down' drug, I didn't particularly enjoy it, but I think that's getting more common as a means of getting over the evening. There is such a shift in environment from being in a club where everything is on the move and adjusting from that to being still or thoughtful, and smack is a shortcut to making the leap from one stage to another.
>
> (Ruth)

Female clubbers were also very aware of the negative aspects of taking drugs and recognized that even in a recreational setting, people could move into the realms of more problematic drug use. Anne also highlights that she did not like going in search of drugs:

> Quite early on a small group of people became quite affected by drugs it changed them as people and created a lot of problems in their lives. I think that was the first taste it wasn't as fun and innocent as it should be. I didn't like having to scoot about trying to find drugs.
>
> (Anne)

It was also observed that alcohol is starting to become more apparent on club scenes.

> I think alcohol is returning to things but I think that's because people can't get decent quality ecstasy, I think people burnt themselves out so they've gone back to drinking. Britain's culture is very drink-orientated so I think that's inevitable really.
>
> (Chris)

For female clubbers alcohol made them act in an unsafe, out of control way, and it was seen as a destructive and damaging substance. By contrast, using ecstasy and dance drugs meant that an element of control could be maintained therefore reducing the risks of being out in club spaces. 'Alice' is clear about this distinction between alcohol and drug-related risks:

---

5   It must be noted that alcohol is the most prevalent substance used in drink-spiking.

I don't think personally that there is a problem with recreational drug use, there's more of a problem with alcohol use. Statistics show there are more alcohol-related incidents than drugs-related. Going out, drinking twenty pints, lying in a gutter with head injuries, I think that's a lot more serious than taking an illegal substance and having a bit more control over what you're doing.

(Alice)

Clubbers such as 'Alice' see alcohol as a substance that produces more risky behaviour, both in themselves and others. Club spaces are licensed premises and the re-emergence of alcohol as a drug of choice, which is linked in turn to a resurgence in the use of cocaine, means that alcohol is likely to be consumed in addition to illegal drugs such as ecstasy, cocaine and amphetamines. Thus the spaces used for clubbing are more dangerous in terms of risk, as alcohol is a substance that is linked with violence and inappropriate behaviour by men. It is also a substance that female clubbers stated made them behave in less responsible, more risky ways. The significance of the risks taken by female clubbers is associated with pleasure, as well as the types of clubs they socialized in, and the social rules governing behaviour in these different spaces.

Investigation around the source of the drugs taken by female clubbers showed that it was mainly from friends or 'friends of friends' that ecstasy was obtained, not from the stereotypical, dangerous, unscrupulous male dealer. Women clubbers rarely had a bad experience from the physical effects of the drugs themselves and the experience of taking ecstasy was couched in terms of an exciting, enhancing, pleasurable experience and as part of a social event with friends. The only bad thing identified about using ecstasy and other drugs such as amphetamine was the 'comedown'. This refers to the physical and emotional effects from taking drugs during the following one or two days. Tiredness and mild anxiety or depression are associated with the comedown period, and for some respondents it is more extreme. This is the reason why they argue that they have cut down or stopped their use of ecstasy. 'Irina' described her drug usage:

It's less important as I've got older. I take less now as I stopped for a while 'cos I was getting really paranoid and I'm sure it was to do with the drugs I was taking, so I actually took none for two years.

(Irina)

A theme which has been reinforced in this discussion is the idea of risk and safety. To outsiders women's behaviour may seem to involve risks, and it is true that not all women clubbers act to reduce risk, but in reality female clubbers feel that they are behaving in a way that reduces their risk factors, or that they are making choices that particular types of risk are better than others. Risks are the outcome of sociocultural processes (Lupton 1999) which means female clubbers decide what risks are worth taking and which ones are not depending on their social and cultural position. This reducing or weighing up of risk for women is illustrated in the ways they usually buy their drugs, from trusted dealers who they know or from friends. The theme of risk and safety can be further developed in the context of the differences between *mainstream* and *underground* club spaces. Risk associated with drug use and harassment by men is reduced in *underground* clubs, as is the risk associated with buying drugs because generally the dealer is someone who is known to the women clubbers concerned. However risk in the use of illegal substances is still apparent and never disappears completely, so it is always associated with the clubbing lifestyle, however well it is managed.

Pleasure and Drug Use

Drug use is explicitly linked to notions of pleasure, risk, danger and sex and the use of drugs, especially ecstasy is often portrayed in the media as producing wild, abandoned sexual behaviour amongst young women (Williamson 1997). These stereotypical images of 'pleasure seeking' women need to be reassessed with a focus instead on how female clubbers view their own behaviour. The effects of drugs such as ecstasy lower inhibitions in relation to sexual practices (Henderson 1996), and attitudes towards these lowered inhibitions reflect ideas about age and naïvety expressed by female clubbers in relation to sexually inexperienced younger women. Younger less experienced clubbers were seen to be more at risk from the effects of these lowered inhibitions. It was felt that younger women might not be able to cope with more experienced and seductive older men, or with incidents of harassment. As 'Erica' put it:

> If there's somebody you just keep away from them like that mad dancing guy, there's like the odd character or you tend to pick up on a vibe and keep away from them, but I think younger girls who are new on the scene it might be different.
>
> (Erica)

'Anne' also expressed fears for younger women who are less experienced:

> Yeah casual sex and ecstasy ... Younger women might feel a sense of pressure and feel that you can't go home with someone and not have sex. It doesn't trouble me personally although I do recognize the inequality.
>
> (Anne)

And 'Sheila' described how:

> You do see women letting it all hang out, maybe it isn't actually that they feel any pressure to do it, but I think these things can be very subtle because especially younger women really who are wanting to get boyfriends and be attractive are looking at what the standards are, what are the attractive girls that get the attention and how are they dressed, how are they behaving.
>
> (Sheila)

Women clubbers in discussing their own sexual feelings stated that if they did feel like having sex it was after the club when they were 'coming down' from the drugs used. While they were in the club dancing and socializing, sex was not in the forefront of their minds. Although a couple of women said that they had had one-off sexual experiences whilst in the club, this was not usual practice either on *mainstreams* or *undergrounds*. The general consensus was that while out at a club on ecstasy you did feel 'touchy' and 'huggy' as a result of the effects of the drug, but not sexual. This was seen as part of the 'pleasure' element of taking drugs and most of the female clubbers stated that ecstasy made them feel sexy, but not like having sex. Some especially enjoyed this sexy feeling when out with partners which progressed to intercourse or other kinds of sexual behaviour when they got home *after* clubbing, in their 'comedown' stage. Such an experience is described as:

> Its really horny being with (names partner), I'll kind of hold onto him, cuddle him and stuff, it feels gorgeous, but it's usually when I get home I'm even more horny!
>
> (Alex)

Another description of the way ecstasy heightens feeling sexy is:

> It makes me feel affectionate, I wouldn't say it always makes me feel sexual, I feel physical and attractive, so yeah, I suppose in that way, but not you know.
>
> (Chris)

'Rave' culture is seen as less focused around sexual gratification (Henderson 1996; McRobbie 1994) and while it is certainly true that at the dance event itself, overt sexual behaviour is put aside for friendliness and mingling with strangers, it is *after* the club event that sexual encounters take place, often with people met at the event. Club scenes do not have the conventional approach to sex and sexuality found at alcohol-based clubs,[6] but this does not mean that a discourse about sex and sexuality is not present. To state club scenes are less focused around sexual gratification is to oversimplify a more complex situation as clubs' spaces are not necessarily an avoidance of sexuality (Skelton and Valentine 1998). Female clubbers stated that sex is likely to occur later on in the experience of taking ecstasy in the 'comedown' period and Thompson in Saunders (1997) found that three out of four users had practised sex while under the influence of ecstasy. However a shift in the emphasis on sexual behaviour could also be due to the changes in drug use that have occurred within club spaces. By 1994, due to the bad quality of ecstasy it was not the predominant drug used by clubbers, and drugs such as cocaine, amphetamine and alcohol were more popular. Therefore a sexual vibe and an emphasis on sexual behaviour were more apparent than they had been in purely ecstasy-based club nights.[7]

What is notable in discussions with female clubbers about sexualities and sexual behaviour are the alternative discourses on female desire and pleasure they reveal.

---

6   Alcohol-based clubs were seen by the women interviewed as being 'meat markets' for men to pick up women. Club scenes where ecstasy was the main drug used were seen as having a better attitude towards relations between the sexes, where picking up women for sex was not the main agenda for the men attending.

7   It must be noted here that the quality of the ecstasy is variable and this has effects on club spaces as the ethos and atmosphere changes according to the drugs used.

Clubbing women felt that they were moved to respond to desire and pleasure in a different way and when sex and ecstasy had been mixed it was a much more intense experience, but that they failed to reach orgasm. Thus a *different* pleasure is had by being able to indulge in long or different periods of sexual behaviour. For example oral sex may be more common as ecstasy tends to inhibit orgasm in both men[8] and women. This could also mean that sexual encounters were less risky, although stimulant drugs can contribute to long periods of penetrative sex resulting in damage or irritation to the vaginal and anal tissue. The fact that pleasure was different was attributed to the effects of ecstasy on the body, making touch and sexual experiences much more sensual. Sheila described her sexual experience as:

> More memorable, better I don't know, 'cos I wouldn't say I'm only going to have sex on ecstasy. It was just different, it was intense, very intense in a way that only having sex on drugs can be.
>
> (Sheila)

Sophie accounted for the effect of drugs on the experience of orgasm as:

> I think being on ecstasy and having sex, your concept of time is completely different, the pleasure seems to go on for much longer, much more intensively. I still find it really difficult to come on E in fact I don't think I've ever managed it actually!
>
> (Sophie)

Some female clubbers also stated that mixing sex and ecstasy made their sex lives better as it meant that their male partners would not reach orgasm as quickly if at all. This was experienced as especially liberating for some female clubbers who enjoyed the enhanced sexual pleasures this resulted in. Engaging in more significant and varied sexual behaviours can also be analysed as a form of resistance to the dominant discourse on passive female sexuality. This is affirmed by 'Cynthia' as:

> Generally it makes the bloke last longer which can enhance things from my point of view definitely! Most of the time when I go out and take ecstasy you end up back at somebody's house staying up all night so I very rarely have sex when I'm up, it's in the morning when you're coming down.
>
> (Cynthia)

Female clubbers felt that sex on ecstasy was not better than 'sober' sex, just different, even if it was more intense. They also stated that the freeing of inhibitions around body image was a very positive experience when mixing sex and ecstasy, which made these experiences very pleasurable. The following quotes highlight some of the ways women clubbers can experience positive expressions of female sexualities when mixing sex and drugs. Freeing themselves from negative body image constraints was a pleasurable experience which challenges dominant ideologies of femininity as passive and subordinate:

---

8   The use of ecstasy in men can also inhibit erection (Meesham et al. 2000).

I met this bloke on the scene and the relationship was based around using ecstasy and stuff, so in that sense we had really good sex, but I think you're more uninhibited because you're absolutely off your head and you go with your feelings more.

(Irina)

I definitely need to relax as I'm too uptight about how my body looks, and the way this, that and the other looks. When I'm pilled up (under the influence of ecstasy) I don't give a shit, so it's all just the sensation and horny when you're pilled up.

(Alex)

Female clubbers also commented that the amount of pleasure involved in mixing sex and drugs can be emphasized as parts of the body become more sensitive when drugs such as ecstasy are used. Using ecstasy makes touching and physical contact much more sensational. This partly accounts for that way that female clubbers felt 'sexy', but not like having sex when they were 'luved up'. This is summed up by 'Irina':

It really depended on the kind of drug it was 'cos sometimes you could feel really sensual, like any touch was unbelievable.

(Irina)

Safer Sexual Behaviour and Drug Use

Sexual behaviour and drug use are constructed through notions of danger and risk. An exploration of how women keep themselves from harm when negotiating sexual encounters whilst using drugs has implications for HIV and STD prevention, which are twofold: firstly it raises issues as to whether using ecstasy makes it more likely that young women will indulge in unsafe sexual behaviour, and secondly whether unsafe sexual behaviour is more likely to occur in this social setting, than in other settings among other social groups (Henderson 1993). The use of drugs in relation to sexual behaviour is complicated by cultural expectations as well as the pharmacological effects of the drugs themselves. 'Copping off' (leaving the venue with a partner for sex) on club scenes is not seen as a major consideration, since most sexual encounters occur after the club, in a casual way. However, when sex occurs after the club in this way, there is a certain unprepared or unexpectedness to it, so condom use may not be a consideration (Henderson 1993).

Whilst on the one hand pleasure, sexuality and recreational drug use are positively linked by female clubbers, there is another more risky side to the concoction. Drug use is not an underlying factor in whether young women indulge in unsafe sex and it is alcohol rather than drug use that is more likely to result in risky behaviour (Henderson 1996). Women clubbers stated that they were still aware of safer-sex issues when mixing sex and drugs, but that they could see how others would not be. Although clubbers attributed this to a tendency that if people were less concerned about safer sex, they were less stringent in practising it in all situations and using drugs made no difference at all to their behaviour. 'Risky' behaviour needs to be explored within the context of world views which may differ greatly from that of the 'expert' risk assessor or 'outsider' (Fox 1999). So for women clubbers the decisions they make about risk are taken within their own particular world view about what is acceptable and what is not. The following quotes emphasize the risks associated with pleasure linked to drug taking and sexual behaviour. 'Ruth' and 'Cynthia' take risks with sexual health in all their sexual encounters, but some risks such as pregnancy are seen as unacceptable to take, whilst others such as sexually transmitted diseases are seen as less important.

> Yes I'm very aware of the issues but I tend to be a bit slack on them anyway so I don't really think it makes any difference. There's been situations where safe sex has been something I've had to think about, I haven't ever thought stuff it, forget it.
>
> (Cynthia)

> Er, oops, yes I'm aware of the issues but I take other precautions, safe sex in terms of getting pregnant I'm very aware of, but safe sex in terms of STDs (sexually transmitted diseases) tends to take a back seat, which is a negative side of it.
>
> (Ruth)

One of the inherent dangers in engaging in casual sex in an unprepared way after being out clubbing is the pressure to have unsafe sex. Women clubbers were quite happy to have sex in a casual way, and most were clear that this had to be safe sex involving condom use. It was their male counterparts who were prepared to take risks in relation to sexual safety, and this meant that women had to be assertive to protect their sexual health. 'Jackie' expresses this in the lack of male awareness of safe sex and condom use:

> It depends who I'm with, I've found that a lot of blokes are rubbish at safe sex, which I feel shocked about in a way. I thought that everybody had safe sex, but it seems like nobody does. I know it's nowhere near as panic driven as it was about HIV, but I've been sleeping around quite a bit recently and out of say five guys only one of them initiated condom use which is pretty bad. I can't believe they don't know how to put one on, all the women they must have been out with, its like 'oh God'!
>
> (Jackie)

This however could introduce an element of danger as refusal to have sex without a condom risked an aggressive response from the men concerned. As 'Naomi' described:

> The idea was that we would go back to his and have sex, and I didn't have a problem with that, but he didn't have any condoms and I didn't have any condoms so I said 'sorry mate, your names not on the list so you're not coming in!' He got really, really angry about it.
>
> (Naomi)

Therefore casual sexual encounters in the context of club spaces as in any other area of everyday life carry a certain amount of risk and for clubbing women there is also a limited time to assess the risk involved so being in control and not making bad judgements were important to female clubbers. There was also a shared view that alcohol far more than drugs made women take risks, not just sexually but in every aspect of going out. 'Anne' stated that:

> I have been in situations where I've not wanted to have sex with someone and have had to say no, but I've always been in a position where that's said. I was talking about having a sense of control, and I feel a lot more sense of control when I've been in that situation when I'm on drugs than when I'm drunk.
>
> (Anne)

As 'Bella' illustrates, when alcohol was consumed judgements about safer sex and condom use were also seen to be blurred.

> I suppose if I went out to a club and got drunk I'd be more likely to have sex without thinking about what I'm doing, when you've had E you're still aware of everything, but when you're pissed you're not.
>
> (Bella)

Women clubbers therefore reported that taking ecstasy made them retain more control over their sexual encounters and to be more assertive about safer sex and condom use than when they were under the influence of alcohol. As 'Cynthia' concluded:

> I think maybe it puts you more in a situation where you're willing to say 'right let's use a condom' than if you were completely straight, you might get to a stage where you don't want to mention it.
>
> (Cynthia)

Risk, Self-Esteem and the Expectations of Others

Female clubbers were clear that as they had got older, more assertive and had more confidence and self esteem, they would simply not put up with irresponsible behaviour from men, and felt able to stand up for their rights. The major factors in determining condom use and low-risk behaviour are levels of confidence and self esteem (Henderson 1996). The notion of taking risks and pleasure linked to danger are emphasized when the female clubbers concerned have low self-confidence and low self-esteem. When clubbing women did have low self-confidence and low self-esteem they were not able to articulate their needs, or initiate condom use, so risk-taking behaviour becomes routine. This is cogently expressed by 'Alex' who felt that:

> I used to get really, really fucked all the time and not look after myself. My self-esteem has improved having done my college course, and my life changing. Last year I was shagging (having sex with) this guy, we'd take pills, drink loads of alcohol and he never used anything, so I was really daft, but I think that's intermingled with the fact that I wasn't really happy about myself so I didn't really give a shit about myself.
>
> (Alex)

'Irina' described her experience as:

> Difficult in the sense that you wish you hadn't done it! I've never been in a situation that
> I've slept with someone I didn't want to, but sometimes afterwards I've thought 'fucking
> hell how empty was that' and not felt particularly brilliant about it.
>
> (Irina)

The experiences of female clubbers also showed that there could be misconceptions around drug use and sexual inhibitions. Whilst the use of ecstasy might make women feel more sensual and wanting to engage in some types of sexual activity, intercourse may not be a desired outcome, which in turn could lead to surprise or indignation on their partner's side. This is illuminated by 'Cynthia' in the following quote:

> I think people would be surprised if you turned round and said 'no I'm not interested',
> 'cos they might think you've had an E and you'd be more inclined to jump into bed with
> people. I think most people I know would be surprised if I turned down sex, under any
> circumstances! I don't personally feel pressure but I think it's generally expected. I think
> if you went home with somebody they'd be incredibly surprised if you weren't willing to
> have intercourse.
>
> (Cynthia)

Even though clubbing women stated that their sexual experiences could be more significant and experimental when using ecstasy the expectation here is that penetrative sex will still take place. Therefore the expectations of others about the behaviour of women who have taken ecstasy are significant in the negotiation of sexual encounters. Despite the openness and freedom associated with club spaces women are still constrained by traditional images of how they should behave and are treated accordingly, even though male clubbers are supposedly 'a bit more aware of feminism' (Jackie, female clubber).

The Ecstasy and the Agony: Doing Drugs and Sex

The effects of drug usage therefore are complicated by the expectations held by others about the likely behaviour of women who have taken drugs such as ecstasy. Female clubbers using some club spaces are no longer subjected to overt pressure and harassment by men, but this has become much more covert and subtle, and ingrained within the social rules of different club scenes. The level of subtlety differs between *mainstream* and *underground* club spaces, but even when women clubbers stated that they did not feel pressured into having sex, they acknowledged that this pressure existed, especially for younger women who had not yet learned the rules, or how to confront them. 'Naomi' described this pressure to have sex in an incident she recounted:

> Because I'd taken a lot of speed, I was sat up in bed with him and he would keep trying to
> shag me. I was just waiting for daylight so I could say 'fuck off I'm going home now'!
>
> (Naomi)

Club scenes are important sexually for women as they do not have the constraints on their sexuality that are found in other social spaces such as pubs for example. In club spaces sexual choices are increased with the use of ecstasy and other club drugs which leads to a blurring of sexual identities making experimentation acceptable within some *undergrounds*. On the other hand within *mainstreams* this 'liberal' atmosphere regarding sexual behaviour acts in a detrimental way towards young women by increasing the pressures on them to have sex in a casual way through attitudes towards sexuality. This is not to argue that equality and respect are always apparent in *undergrounds* and that women never suffer from harassment in these spaces. Therefore contemporary club spaces still involve women clubbers negotiating the pleasurable experiences of their sexuality within the constraints that 'open-ness' about sexuality leads to. Unfortunately the use of ecstasy in clubs was also highlighted as giving men an excuse to push things 'one step further' in terms of harassment or pressuring women to have sex, with the explanation that they were 'off their heads'. In an alarming way club scenes and drug using culture provided men with an environment to push their behaviour to the limits without taking any responsibility for the consequences, and without considering the effects on the women concerned. 'Alex' recognized this in her view that 'I think it's a code in clubs that when you're pilled up you're supposed to not mind if someone comes up, gives you a hug or touches and stuff like that'. 'Ruth' gave her opinion that 'I can imagine people being more vulnerable (through the use of ecstasy) and there are certain people who will play on that vulnerability'.

The social rules concerning touching, hugging and massaging meant that women clubbers could not object to behaviour they felt crossed a certain line. This leaves them open to covert harassment by men as it is legitimized by the unspoken rules of the club spaces concerned. As 'Alex' put it:

> The first time I'd taken a pill in Manchester this guy was kneading my back, touching me and I just wasn't comfortable. I was like who are you and I don't know how to get away from this, you're expected to not mind
>
> (Alex)

So whilst it is argued (Meesham et al. 2000, Hunt and Evans 2003) that women face less sexual harassment from men in club spaces the female clubbers presented here stated that these unspoken rules meant that they had to accept intimate touch that was sometimes unwanted. Sexual harassment is still apparent but it is expressed within the social rules of club spaces more covertly and subtly than in alcohol based spaces. Although female clubbers described difficult situations in relation to sexual pressure some women partially blamed good quality drugs for their bad judgements about who to have sex with and spoke about the consequences in a humorous way.

> I stopped gratuitously snogging people! There must have been some incredibly good Es around and twice in a month I took awful men home, just because I thought they were the

most fantastic snog alive, but actually it was just because I was off my face and anyone would have been a fantastic snog!

(Sophie)

There were only a few incidents of actual violence or threat of violence coming to the fore, which had tragic consequences for the women involved, as 'Cynthia' illustrates:

That was blamed on drugs in a very large way (a rape that occurred one night after clubbing, by a friend's boyfriend who claimed he didn't know what he was doing because he was 'off his head'). Something that irritated me about that whole partying and drug scene was the idea that you can turn it into a seventies orgy scene, where everyone just paws everyone else, and saying no but still having things pressured onto you because hey, 'you're off your head'.

(Cynthia)

'Cynthia' also implies here that the social rules governing some club spaces and attitudes mean that female clubbers are expected to cope with entirely unacceptable and morally reprehensible behaviour from some male clubbers. Thus, the social rules of clubbing mean that some men get away with relinquishing responsibility for violent and abusive behaviour. 'Naomi' described how, when being intimate with a female friend, they were harassed by men attending the same club night:

We were holding hands and kissing and him and his mate came over and tried to get off with us and we weren't having any of it, that was very threatening because of what he said to us and the way that he couldn't accept whatever he thought our sexual relationship was, he couldn't deal with it because it offended his macho pride. I didn't feel safe to take drugs until the threat was removed, he scared the shit out of me.

(Naomi)

This particular experience emphasizes that heterosexuality is taken as the norm in society and this norm is closely linked to the use of spaces and places within club scenes. Sexual identities in particular are not always static, but women are judged by their *appearance* to fit into one category or another. Lesbians who are clear about not being sexually available to men are subject to harassment because they stand out as different. However it is not only lesbian women who find such approaches by men unwanted, this is also true for heterosexual women. Women in general experience anti-lesbian abuse simply because they are not interested in the men concerned. This abuse is therefore used to police independent women's behaviour *whatever* their sexuality may be. Differences between women on club scenes can make identifying homogeneous groups very difficult for participants. For example, women who identify as heterosexual but do not perform their gender in a 'desirable' way such as 'Naomi', encounter harassment in the form of anti-lesbian abuse. In a similar vein 'feminine lesbians' can be taken as heterosexual. In these cases you do not have to *be* one you just have to *look like* one to be seen as a threat (Valentine 1996) so for female clubbers in terms of their sexualities they still have to conform and 'look right' to avoid censure and harassment.

The use of recreational drugs by women can be both a source of pleasure and risk. It must be recognized that women gain pleasure from clubbing and using drugs and this needs to be looked at in conjunction with the risks involved. Pleasure was derived from avoiding risk and being in control despite being under the influence of drugs such as ecstasy. Also pleasure was found in the friendly, social atmosphere of underground club spaces, and in spending time there with friends. On the whole female clubbers felt that they suffered from less harassment on ecstasy-based underground scenes, and this was a positive aspect, as they could 'let their hair down' without fear of reprisals. Sexually, clubbing was a source of pleasure as the *attitude* in some spaces meant that women were able to be proactive and assertive about whom to have sex with. Women were seen as having a right to be visible, pleasure seeking and having fun.

It must be noted though that even in the more open environment of club spaces, women clubbers struggle with conceptions of femininity and how to express themselves without inviting censure. Women within club spaces may view their sexuality and sexual behaviour quite radically, but in contemporary society it is still problematic for women to express their sexuality whatever it is and club spaces are no different in this respect. Some types of clubbing spaces are seen as safer than others allowing female sexualities to be negotiated within wider boundaries and with more freedom. Male attitudes and subsequent behaviour are also an important factor in how 'free' women attending feel to express their identities. Therefore negotiating sexuality within club spaces is risky for women, but the extent to which problems occur is connected to issues of difference between clubs defined as *mainstreams* and *undergrounds*. *Mainstreams* were seen by female clubbers as involving more risk than *undergrounds*, both in the performance of sexuality and in engaging in sexual behaviour. Men with negative attitudes towards women's sexuality were seen to congregate in *mainstream* spaces, while more positive male attitudes were seen as related to *undergrounds*.

The quote by 'Naomi' identified earlier further highlights one aspect of risk and club scenes, which is linked to displaying ambiguous, lesbian or bisexual identities. The female clubbers involved in this incident take a greater risk by choosing to be open in their sexuality, than if their behaviour had been heterosexual. Heterosexual women are more visible in some spaces because of the emphasis on their sexuality, so lesbian women face a 'double risk' in being open in mainstream spaces. This aspect of participating in club spaces is focused on in chapter five, which examines safety within different club spaces and in the city, as well as exploring tolerance towards the expression of different sexualities.

Chapter 5

Safety, Sexuality in the Club and in the City

Introduction

In this chapter the issues of safety both inside club spaces and outside in negotiating the city at night will be explored in more depth. In both settings the negotiation of sexualities and gender are at the core of how comfortable women clubbers feel. How women relate to their own and others shifting identities is an important issue as spaces and places are not gendered in themselves, but they both reflect and affect the ways in which gender is constructed and understood (Massey 1994). Although women still face constraints on their use of the city as a site of leisure (Stanko 1990, 1997), their position in contemporary society has changed. Therefore the significance of viewing contested spaces in terms of identity construction and consumption practices is important in the wider context of the club spaces. Sexual diversity and freedom are often portrayed as particularly urban phenomena, leading to minority sexual subcultures and communities being more developed in cities (Bell and Valentine 1995). Whilst club spaces may be perceived as 'safe', the outside world of the city at night is still perceived as dangerous by lesbian, bisexual and heterosexual women. However, by taking part in the city at night these women subvert the 'unsafeness' in the same way that lesbian action groups, for example, subvert the heterosexuality of 'everyday' spaces (Valentine 1996). Thus heterosexuality as well as gender is the dominant force controlling city spaces and places, and the system of heteronormality regulates all women regardless of how they see their sexual identities (Valentine 1996). It is both the risks and pleasures of finding a place in the night time economy of the city that is focused upon in this chapter.

Feeling safe for female clubbers depended on who they were with and where they were. Issues of safety and sexuality were experienced differently depending on the space that was being negotiated as there was an understanding of certain mainstream clubs as 'meat markets', where male attitudes to women were predatory and sexist. In such places there was higher consumption of drugs such as amphetamine and cocaine and the music was more 'hardcore'.[1] These factors contributed to an aggressive *attitude* and to a less friendly atmosphere toward those attending. Women

---

1   Hardcore is a term that refers to a particular type of techno music that has a high number of beats per minute.

experienced these spaces in terms of a more intimidating, aggressive *attitude* from the men who used these clubs. Underground club spaces where the music policy was more experimental or 'breakbeat'[2] were seen as much more friendly spaces with better attitudes both in relation to women and towards others in general. Female clubbers preferred nights that were not as frenetic and 'hardcore', and preferred to socialize in more friendly club spaces that made them feel safer.

Safety Inside Club Spaces

An important issue for discussion is how safe women clubbers felt once they had reached their destination; the club of their choice. Less sexist attitudes are assumed to exist in places where ecstasy is used but this is not the case for all club spaces. Female clubbers stated that they felt safe inside the places they went to, and feeling safe was linked to *attitude*, which is the most important defining factor in how women clubbers chose their involvement in club spaces. The *attitudes* of those attending contributed to the atmosphere and if this became threatening female clubbers stated that it would force them to leave, as it undermined the ethos of participating in club spaces. Part of the ethos behind participating in club spaces for women is that they are freed from certain constraints around their behaviour and feel that they are participating in a less sexist environment. 'Irina' recounted that:

> Some of the clubs are quite male dominated and there does seem to be a bit more of an edge than there used to be. Nothing ever happened, but I just don't feel as comfortable there as I have been in the past, thinking there may be a possibility for violence.
>
> (Irina)

'Feeling safe' was a sensation that was experienced for many women in gay clubs in comparison to straight clubs.

> This sounds really heterosexist, but I don't think I'd go to a straight club while I was off my head, I do think I feel safer in a gay club. It seems that the likelihood of going into a straight place and finding an argument or a fight happens a lot more than it would in a gay club.
>
> (Lucy)

For women clubbers apart from some minor incidents on the dance floor such as men dancing too close to them, their clubbing careers had been very safe.

---

2 Breakbeat evolved from late 1980s rave and its attributes are 'funky rhythm tracks, lots of samples and choppy mixes, sped-up "chipmunk" vocal loops, frenetic explosive energy with a speed of 135 to 170 beats per minute' (www.ethnotechno.com.defs.php). Breakbeat music is the sampling of breaks as drum loops (beats) and using them as a basis for hip hop tunes for example. More contemporary electronic artists and club DJs have created 'breakbeats' from other electronic music and fused them together. So this type of music is literally composed by 'breaking the beats' of other songs (http://en.wikipedia.org/wiki/breakbeat).

Assertiveness and feeling confident were key factors in deterring men who might be persistent in unwanted sexualized behaviour. Clubbing women felt they were part of the spaces they socialized in, as they contributed to the atmosphere of the night, just by attending, taking drugs and dancing. They felt the scene(s) belonged to them and were comfortable taking part in these spaces and their rituals. This may account for female clubbers feeling more assertive when it came to dealing with unwanted attention from men, as they felt their right to enjoy themselves was being undermined. Women are no longer accepting their marginal position within social spaces such as clubs, and a new assertiveness has developed linked to the expression of sexuality and saying 'no' to unwanted sexual advances by men. Female clubbers feel that they have a 'right' to say no and to challenge unwanted sexualized behaviour by men. Thus for some clubbers the notion of being female is linked to the idea of feeling powerful and being a 'can do' girl (Harris 2004) can also be described in terms of female clubbers attitudes towards their own femininities and sexualities. 'Sophie' is quite clear about how to deal with unwanted advances:

> I'm a very straight up assertive person. I've been able to deal with them and perhaps someone who wasn't as assertive would have had more trouble. I've been able to say 'I'm not going to have sex with you' quite early on which a lot of people might find difficult to say.
>
> (Sophie)

One aspect of feeling safe for female clubbers was linked to controls exerted by supportive others on their sexual behaviour. Friends took on a role in controlling women's sexual behaviour as, for example, 'unsuitable' men are not tolerated and friends are steered away from them. Women look on each other as a safety net when getting home at night and would not leave clubs to go home alone without their friends. Female clubbers recognize that they are still constrained by the attitudes of those outside club spaces and that their 'liberation' does not automatically extend to the spaces of the street. As 'Ruth' states:

> I think you have to be more careful, women have got to look out for themselves. You don't go home on your own and you don't go home with a bloke you've met that night unless you've got your mates with you.
>
> (Ruth)

As friends who arrive together go home together for safety reasons this sticking together also limits sexual access to women by men in club spaces. So for women engaging in risk taking behaviour in the context of clubbing their behaviour had a safety net as their female friends 'watch their back'. Women clubbers also felt much more comfortable flirting and dancing with men on ecstasy based underground club spaces, knowing that this behaviour would not be misinterpreted as readily. Men participating in club spaces who were using the same drugs largely had similar attitudes towards being flirtatious. As 'Alice' describes:

You can tell if someone's on drugs quite easily, and if they know you're on drugs they behave in a certain very friendly way. One of the things about it is you don't really get that meat market thing at the types of clubs I go to, you don't go round chatting people up, people mix in a lot more platonic way, you can dance and flirt and it's not a problem.

(Alice)

Women participating in club spaces are involved in assessing risk relating to sexual encounters. If they did want to 'cop off' (leave the venue with someone for sex) this was seen to be a more equal opportunity to engage in within certain club spaces. In general it was viewed as being safer to initiate sexual encounters in *underground* club spaces that were based around the use of ecstasy, rather than *mainstream* clubs that were perceived as much riskier, based around the use of amphetamines, alcohol and cocaine with an emphasis on sexualized behaviour. These differences relate to both drug use and *attitude*. 'Gail' describes the more equal environment in *undergrounds*. 'People are equally up for it! If people are looking around for someone to cop off with then on the whole it's fairly equal, rather than the boy gets girl thing'. On the other hand women clubbers felt mainstream club spaces were where oppressive attitudes towards women could be found and they preferred to avoid such experiences. As illustrated by 'Gail' it was felt that there was a sexual tension in *mainstream* spaces, that was seen to be lacking in *undergrounds*:

It was dreadful, you got onto the dance floor and hands just grabbed at you from all directions, blokes just going round groping women in an outrageous way, it was really offensive.

(Gail)

During their clubbing careers, women can be seen to move from *mainstreams* to *undergrounds*. This can be attributed to the effects of age and experience as younger teenage women are largely unaware of *undergrounds* because they have not been involved with club scenes long enough to 'discover' them.[3] Older female clubbers became disillusioned with *mainstream* clubs quite quickly and moved onto *undergrounds* as places where they felt the *attitude* was more conducive to safe, fun clubbing experiences. 'Alex' sums up this movement in terms of difference:

The difference between clubs, like those I would have gone to in my first year of clubbing, I would have felt less safe with guys mainly drinking and being out of order, than I would in a 'club' club, a proper one!

(Alex)

In terms of better less sexualized attitudes towards women some female clubbers felt there was an absence of sexism in underground club spaces and that they felt very comfortable clubbing in this environment. Others stated that women were treated in a *more* equal way than within alcohol-based mainstream clubs, even though there

---

3 As club fashion and music are more popularized this movement may become less apparent.

were still unequal attitudes prevailing beneath the surface. 'Chris' indicated the contrast of experiences in mainstream and underground clubs:

> I think they get a better deal than they do on the straight (mainstream) scene because on the straight (mainstream) scene we are viewed as meat. Where I go out there isn't much of that, you could sit down with a man, have a conversation without him sticking his tongue down your throat. It's just not done to act in such an ostensibly sexist way towards women, I think its still there but it's not obvious.
>
> (Chris)

'Jessica' agreed that different spaces produced different experiences:

> Yeah for sure compared to a normal club (refers to *mainstreams*). Partly due to some of the politics that are involved in it which are in theory based on equality and people are getting together because they're into it, then those kind of gender differences are taken as seen. Also the absence of leching men, there doesn't seem to be that 'oh right let's stand around and stare at that woman with her tits bouncing'!
>
> (Jessica)

Therefore sexism and harassment of women at underground clubs is not overt and men are censured for 'uncool' behaviour such as being overtly sexist and breaking the social rules of club spaces. There is a general level of harassment that is seen as normal for women in society and club scenes are only a toned down or diluted version of this. The same could be said about sexual safety and the absence of predatory men; that the experience in underground spaces is seen as *relative* to mainstream 'meat market' club spaces. Overt sexism and harassment are plainly not tolerated within underground scenes, as men who behave in this way are censored by the social rules operating in these spaces:

> (names friend) had this top on that flashed and people were smiling and laughing about it. This guy came up and starting gyrating at her and we just shut him out by dancing round her so he couldn't harass her. If people are being offensive then they get shut out of fun things like that.
>
> (Sophie)

However, this has had the effect of driving such behaviour underground where it is just as pervasive and damaging. As discussed in chapter 4 the social rules that operate in club spaces mean that women are expected to accept unwanted and intimate touch. Sexist and sexualized approaches to women have therefore gone underground and become covert and subtle instead of being the norm. This contradiction is emphasized by women clubbers stating that they did not suffer from harassment on underground club scenes, but then going on to describe an incident of harassment that had occurred when out clubbing. In living with this contradiction the female clubbers concerned are negotiating a level of harassment that is still normal for women in society. In this context small incidents of harassment, such as men dancing too close are seen as not very threatening, and consequently are not taken seriously or conceptualized as harassment. More serious threatening incidents such as the pressure to have unsafe sex or abuse for engaging in same sex affection are exposed for what they are, but even then the female clubbers who reported such incidents argued that being pressured into sexual situations was their fault for not being firm. Women clubbers did not question why they had to be firm in these situations, and assumed responsibility for other people's bad behaviour. Male clubbers made assumptions about the sexual behaviour of women who had taken drugs such as ecstasy, but it was the female clubbers who felt they had to bear the responsibility for these masculine assumptions. As 'Naomi' described:

> There's not as much pressure and there's a greater freedom of choice to a certain extent, I can think of situations where I've been pressured into sexual situations, but I should have laid down the law in the first place.
>
> (Naomi)

'Naomi' does not question why she should have laid down the law in the first place surely 'no' should have been enough? So not only do female clubbers feel pressured into having sex when they do not want to, but they blame themselves for others' lack of responsibility and respect. This type of sexual pressure is not confined to female clubbers, but it seems all the more insidious when the spaces in question are allegedly based on more equal attitudes and respect for others. 'Anne' conceptualizes the harassment women do suffer from:

> I think that a lone woman on the scene (*underground* scenes) stands to get a lot of harassment or lots of attention, so I think while the club scene pretends to be something new and different it isn't at all, as a woman you are in exactly the same place as you were in the city or whatever.
>
> (Anne)

As discussed in chapter 4 women clubbers highlighted that some men on club scenes try to 'push their luck' and take things 'one step further' in a sexual way, as women are seen as an easy target for sex because they have taken ecstasy.[4] This emphasizes the risks that women take when involving themselves in club scenes and engaging in pleasure-seeking behaviour. One of those risks is that they are a target for men whose sexualized behaviour has become more subtle and covert, and who do see women clubbers who have taken drugs as an 'easy lay'. 'Sophie' sees ecstasy as giving an excuse for tactile behaviour:

> I think because of the amount of tactileness that comes out of it (taking ecstasy), men push boundaries further than they normally would, the 'no' barrier might get misunderstood, the 'I'm enjoying this because it's an experience of being tactile and sexy, but that doesn't mean I'm going to have sex with you', may be misunderstood by a man because of the way men think. I've never seen that erupt into anything unpleasant, just hurt egos or

---

4   This is because ecstasy lowers peoples inhibitions and clubbers feel more open and friendly towards strangers.

bewilderment and moving on to the next victim, I keep thinking of (names a particular man) leching after women.

(Sophie)

Therefore, not surprisingly, women clubbers who were heterosexual stated that they felt safer if they had a male partner with them when using club spaces for pleasure and drug taking. 'Because I like having a boyfriend I feel safe if he's around, but I don't feel it's as meat markety as in a straight club' (Chris). Feeling secure in their drug use was enhanced by being able to spend it with someone who was especially close, and emphasized the sensual, pleasurable or 'sexy' feelings that ecstasy use engenders.

When I first come up, I want to dance and there's people around me chatting and dancing. I fuckin' love all that, now I'm with (names partner) and I watch him dancing, I really fancy him and I'll go and dance with him, it's like 'oh fuck'.

(Alex)

Although clubbing women also identified negative factors associated with clubbing and being with a male partner. This highlights that part of what women liked about clubbing and drug use were the risk factors involved. Deviant behaviour such as using drugs is risky, exciting and pleasurable and these issues are often overlooked in classic accounts of crime and deviance. The seductions of crime (Katz 1988) are often seen as unimportant especially for young women. This is not to say that female clubbers courted danger or did not assess risks, but the excitement involved in flirting, dancing and feeling free with strangers was a part of clubbing that was not open to them when male partners were present. As 'Gail' put it:

I always felt constricted (when with a male partner). Clubbing is about lots of different people getting together and feeling free and open. I always felt a bit held back by being with a partner.

(Gail)

'Irina' implied that if they expected their partner to be tolerant of their flirtatious behaviour, it was sometimes difficult to be tolerant in return.

I used to find it hard because people were uninhibited and he was going round hugging people, I used to get a bit jealous, and the other way round because you're more familiar with people.

(Irina)

Therefore, when clubbing, women do not always feel as safe as they should, so being with their male partner can make them feel more secure. This also makes the negotiation of risk involved in taking part in the night time economy easier. The risks associated with taking part in club spaces were seen to be related to how those both outside and within club scenes perceived women who used drugs. However drug use can also adversely affect relationships due to the uninhibited behaviour of either partner or the people around them. Some female clubbers stated that their relationships were solely based around drug use and clubbing, and that they could not relate to partners in any other forum. This meant that drugs and alcohol were used excessively, so they were able to have a 'relationship' and this excessive use of drugs could be destructive and damaging.

Sexuality and Tolerance in Club Spaces

Tolerance of the performance of sexuality in club spaces is related to issues of safety for women. Not only are there issues of safety linked to tolerance for heterosexual women, but also for women who identified as lesbian or bisexual. While heterosexual women were discovered to feel safer when accompanied by a male partner, for women with same sex partners, this could be a different matter.

Clubbing on the gay scene in Manchester was already well developed from the days of disco when 'rave' first hit the city in the late 1980s. For years both gay and straight women had felt comfortable in gay clubs due to the lack of sexual tension between themselves and the gay men that inhabited these spaces (Meesham et al. 2000). So although women may not identify as a lesbian, they feel safer on the gay scene whilst under the influence of drugs, because of an absence of fear of violence or harassment compared to the straight scene. In addition for women crossing over from gay to straight spaces (Ryan and Fitzpatrick 1994), this was more problematic for some than others. How did female clubbers react to displays of same sex affection between other women, and were those engaged in these displays happy to do so in club spaces dominated by heterosexual couples? The answers to these questions depended on the type and location of the club concerned. Underground club spaces were perceived to be more open and cosmopolitan in their attitudes towards a variety of different sexualities, whilst mainstream clubs were approached with caution in relation to expressing lesbian and bisexual identities, or avoided altogether. Using drugs such as ecstasy can be a catalyst for women expressing affection for each other so sexuality can become blurred and ambiguous. Therefore women who are kissing and holding hands may not be lesbian or bisexual, they are expressing their drug-induced heightened feelings through sexualized behaviour. 'Theresa' describes such blurred sexualities:

> When I lived in Manchester I felt I could express sexual feelings towards women quite openly. In (names a town) I feel much more reticent and wary unless I absolutely knew I was in a safe place. People express affection much more freely when they are 'luved up' and two women kissing could be good friends enjoying their drug-induced sexual heightenedness or they could be lovers.
>
> (Theresa)

Other female clubbers were tolerant of expressions of different sexual identities. It was some men who participated in clubbing who were seen as objecting to same sex affection between women in club spaces. It was seen as unacceptable to display same sex affection if the women concerned did not conform to stereotypical images of femininity. Therefore the appearance of the woman or women concerned must be anchored in a performance that is recognized as 'feminine' to be acceptable. Problems arose for women clubbers when lesbian displays of affection were not recognized as 'feminine'. In displaying a lesbian sexuality that was 'real' which showed that the women concerned were not available to men, even if they were desired by them, caused tension and friction in some spaces. At the same time women attending underground club nights were expected to be open minded and tolerant of differences between themselves and others, as it is not only lesbian women who suffer from anti-lesbian abuse. Therefore it is in the interest of all women to combat this type of harassment (Valentine 1996), and this was recognized by women attending club nights as was the right of others to be experimental or different. However, it was felt that in being experimental with sexualities there were inherent dangers. Other female clubbers could mistake being experimental for being experienced and this could lead to difficulties in saying no, as described in the quote below.

> Using 'E' seems to generate more tolerance of the expression of sexual feelings and affection towards other women. This does mean that sexuality can be ambiguous, and women may mistake how you identify your own sexuality. This could lead to difficult situations unless you were clear what your boundaries are.
>
> (Naomi)

With regard to multiple identities and 'fitting in' to different scenes, female clubbers tended to say it was relatively easy to fit in with changing styles in terms of fashion, but with their sexual identities it was obviously much harder. In order to feel comfortable in these situations they had to feel that they blended in and avoided any unwanted attention.

> It can be harder to be yourself in some places, but it's difficult for me to put my finger on why. The thing that affects me most is the other people there, sometimes you can be at a club with a different crowd and feel like you're being looked at oddly and people are being judgmental about you, which makes me feel self conscious.
>
> (Theresa)

Therefore, women who do not identify as heterosexual are likely to be more careful in picking which club spaces to be involved in. The *attitudes* of those attending are seen as an important factor for them to feel comfortable in expressing their sexualities, and they are much more cautious in doing so as fear of violence from men is a constraining factor on non-heterosexual women. Aggression and bad attitudes from other women were rare, and if encountered, even though this was unpleasant, there was not the sexual threat implicit in the same behaviour from men.

Pleasure and Risk in Performing Sexualities

While challenges to sexist stereotyping exist for clubbing women these challenges are hard to articulate. Although the female clubbers discussed here were more assertive than when they were in their teens this does not automatically mean they are happier and more sure of their sexuality. What it does mean is they are in a position to intellectually conceptualize how they feel about these issues. Through good and bad experiences clubbing women had built up a more positive image of female sexuality and were able to express their own sexual identities in these terms. In the quote below 'Sheila' articulates her response to the 'equal' atmosphere on club scenes:

> Women have come a long way as they can go out, take drugs and enjoy themselves. A lot of men used to challenge their attitudes towards women more. New laddism, although you don't associate it with the types of men you get on the club scene, is pervading society. There's still a lot of entrenched sexism, so I don't know if women get any better a deal when it comes to sexism. It could be that women are stronger and will fight for a better deal. But if they're still having to fight to say 'you're wearing a condom mate', then it's just the same. We want men to say 'oh, here are my condoms, we'll use these', and if you still have to persuade them to wash their dick and use a condom, how far have we come since 1971, the female eunuch, Betty Friedan and Kate Millet!
>
> (Sheila)

Therefore women clubbers do derive pleasure from the negotiation of sexualities free from overt harassment from men, and operate with the expectation that others will be tolerant of whatever expression of sexuality and identity they choose to exhibit. However it is not the case that all club spaces are seen as equal and free.

Safety and Traversing the City at Night

While those attending club scenes could be regarded as more accepting of women who are different in dress and sexual behaviour, other men who do not adhere to these social rules have to be negotiated when out in the city at night. Women clubbers felt that whilst they had the freedom to use their leisure opportunities as they wished, there was also an undercurrent of constraints upon that freedom and access to leisure. Clubbing women felt able to choose what to do and where to go, but what constrained them was the negotiation of the city at night. However female clubbers did not avoid the city at night because of risks, they tried to manage these risks instead. Female clubbers, although four were single parents, did not have traditional attitudes towards family responsibilities and did not feel the same gender expectations and constraints attached to these responsibilities. Their responsibilities did not prevent them from taking part in club scenes, or in accessing the city at night, but in doing so they recognized they had to accept a level of danger and risk associated with this. An appreciation of these risks is expressed by 'Erica' who, asked whether she felt safe, said:

No, even before 9pm somebody tried to mug me over there on the way out one night, but if I get a babysitter I'll be out all night and come home at 10 in the morning, so that's fine.

(Erica)

'Cynthia' recognized that safety needed to be negotiated in terms of time and place:

As things go on longer the buses aren't running and that puts you in a position of danger. You find yourself at six in the morning and just think 'oh sod it, I'll walk home'. It depends how I feel on an evening, sometimes I feel invincible and sometimes I feel I just want to be whisked from place to place in a safe little box.

(Cynthia)

The risk of traversing the city at night is linked, as with sexual encounters, to how others perceive women who use drugs. This has an historical basis and is a legacy from nineteenth-century urban cultures in particular the separation of domestic and private spheres (Wilson 1991). This legacy influences the way women are judged by their visibility on the street. In assessing how women experience using the city it is revealed that female clubbers felt they were still targets for harassment by men simply by being visible, in public and out in the city at night, and that this increased the amount of risk they had to negotiate. As 'Evelyn' describes, even taking a taxi, a supposedly 'safe' option, could be fraught with danger as assumptions were made about women who were alone at night.

I don't know if he (taxi driver) thought I was off my head or it was because I was a woman on my own that he thought he could get away with trying it on. He locked me in his taxi, until (names boyfriend) thought it was odd I wasn't getting out and came to see what was going on.

(Evelyn)

Although the city can be seen as a dangerous place for women, where risks have to be assessed and negotiated, it can also be a place of liberation, in that women are free to engage with the pleasures it has to offer (Wilson 1991). This access to the city at night is often at the expense of becoming a target for harassment. Women's fear of violence at the hands of strangers, even if this is unfounded, affects their access to the city as a site of leisure. Female clubbers felt that they were caught in a contradiction; of being free to choose their leisure pursuits in terms of clubbing and using drugs for pleasure, but also of being aware of the censure they face for doing so. The dangers that had to be negotiated to pursue pleasure resulted in tactics and strategies that are particularly gender related. 'Alice' describes her strategy for keeping safe as:

I've never had any incidences where I've felt unsure. I'm good about getting taxis home or going home with a friend. I wouldn't walk home on my own no matter how off it I was.

(Alice)

'Naomi' expressed concern about the safety of her friends as at times they had travelled through unsafe areas of the city, because they lived there.

> There's that kind of no man's land between the comfort of your own home and the comfort of the club. It depends how off your head you are or if you're traveling alone or with friends. I do sometimes feel concerned about friends going to and from places on their own, in the dark, in some unpleasant places.
>
> (Naomi)

Women clubbers were very aware of safety issues when 'out and about' and always tried to ensure that their personal safety was not compromised. Women are more aware of personal-safety issues in relation to public spaces than men (Stanko 1990, 1997) and female clubbers therefore developed strategies to ensure their safety and that of their friends such as taking taxis, or always going home in a group.

> You can always get a taxi and you tend to memorize the taxi ranks, so depending on where you're going you might avoid pub chucking out times, because that's when a lot of aggression is around.
>
> (Naomi)

One aspect of safety was related to style and dress codes. Corporate mainstream clubs that tended to have strict dress codes meant that women were safe within the club as they adhered to the dress code and therefore 'fitted in'. But this 'fitting in' meant their safety was compromised outside when negotiating getting home in an environment where the same dress code could attract unwanted attention from men (see chapter 2 for a discussion of style and dress codes). Some clubs were seen as proactive in these situations by developing their own policies relating to women's safety, as described by 'Alice':

> A couple of women got raped outside (names club); it's very dark down there, and the door men, if you were a single woman or two of you, they had a cab firm that would come and pick you up first, and they would make sure it was an identified cab firm. I know the universities do minibuses and things to get women home safely
>
> (Alice)

An unexpected aspect to the negotiation of risk when using the city at night was that some women felt threatened by the law. This was mainly due to fears about being caught in possession of drugs, and how this would affect their professional careers. Several female clubbers had jobs where they would be sacked immediately with no hope of re-employment anywhere else, if they had a police record for the possession of drugs. 'Ruth' highlights such fears:

> I get cautious about the police if there's lots of you in a car and somebody has got drugs on them. I try not to have them on me because of the other roles in my life, my job, it's quite a big risk really if I did get caught, so I don't feel threatened by people around me I feel threatened by the idea of the law.
>
> (Ruth)

Therefore gender is a crucial factor in looking at spaces in the city and how they are accessed and admittance to city spaces for female clubbers was subject to contradictions. Being out clubbing and taking ecstasy could be a positive experience, but women still had to negotiate risk. For example, stereotypical images of women being out at night had to be carefully navigated to avoid unwanted attention. Having to pass through some city spaces can be extremely difficult even dangerous, with overt harassment by men who consumed alcohol to excess being seen as normal and acceptable. So while overt harassment may not be tolerated in ecstasy-based underground clubs, being out in the city at night can be a perilous undertaking.

Fitting in and Feeling Safe: Negotiating the Right Space

The sense of safety that can accompany the pleasure of clubbing does not extend to all social spaces in club scenes. Female clubbers highlighted that some types of club nights were avoided altogether, due to previous harassment or unfavourable reports from friends. Women are no longer content with being treated solely as girlfriends or sex objects, so they choose club spaces that are conducive to their inclusion. Women symbolically construct spaces as 'safe' through different signifiers such as style and sexuality which are linked to *attitude* (see chapter 2). Accordingly, urban spaces are perceived as gendered and women take for granted that cities such as Manchester are masculinist in nature (Taylor et al. 1996). What women concentrate on are ways of coping with the already established social order and while it can be concluded that female clubbers certainly have fears about personal safety in using the city at night, these do not necessarily constrain them. Women are clear about feeling unsafe, but adopt ways of coping with the threat of male violence. So, for *some* women the city is a site of pleasure, fun and amusement, although the same cannot be said for *all* women, as gender is not a homogenous category. Some city spaces were seen by women clubbers as more male dominated than others, but club spaces tend to be viewed as more equal. This could explain why women find socializing in these spaces pleasurable. As she got older, 'Sophie' felt more able to make choices in relation to being safe:

> It's up to women to know what they want, you avoid places you don't feel comfortable in and you don't play up to what people expect of you. I'm talking as someone who's 30 now and got a lot more self confidence than somebody who was a lot younger and might play up to the scene more.
>
> (Sophie)

For clubbing women it can be concluded that *attitude* differentiates the risk assessment engaged in different club spaces. The different spaces of *mainstreams* and *undergrounds* have different obstacles in relation to safety that have to be negotiated. *Attitude* is therefore an important signifier of how to negotiate these obstacles or risks and this chapter has focused on a discussion of the issues regarding risk and safety for women using club spaces in Manchester. Risks became more or less apparent depending on where participants are physically located, and the *attitudes* of those with whom they were interacting. The way others view women clubbers who use both the city at night and drugs such as ecstasy are important factors which affect the negotiation of safety.

Chapter 6

Consuming and Producing Club Spaces: The Negotiation of Risk and Pleasure by Clubbing Women

A real dick shriveller (ecstasy) it also gets rid of the thinks-with-his-dick mentality, turning rave into a space where girls can feel free to be friendly with strange men, even snog them, without fear of sexual consequences.

(Reynolds in Green 2005, 123)

The notion of club spaces as being a 'luved up', happy environment based on equality and respect has largely been accepted as unproblematic (Malbon 1998; Miles 2000; Pini 2001; Richards and Kruger 1998), and this book has tried to redress the balance with respect to female clubbers and their experiences. Some clubbers and academics alike may feel that I take an unduly pessimistic view of the changes in social spaces that produced the gendered relations discussed in this book. However I wanted to present a picture of the real lived experiences of female clubbers who take part in club spaces and to highlight not only what they found positive about clubbing but also what was risky and problematic for them. It is important to me as a feminist researcher to present the experiences of female clubbers grounded in reality, a reality that does not necessarily gel with the idea of club spaces being places of empowerment. As the experiences of female clubbers show they face harassment and inequality because of their gendered positions within these spaces.

However, despite raising the issues that are risky and problematic for female clubbers there is no denying the pleasures that taking part in club spaces brings them. This is due in part to the *more* equal environment in terms of relations between the sexes. So, whilst it cannot be argued that club spaces are devoid of gendered power relationships they have made some headway into changing these relationships for the better. Female clubbers feel safer, more relaxed and at ease in *undergrounds* where they can explore their identities, take risks, have fun and feel part of a (sub)culture in which they are surrounded by like minded people. What is important about club spaces is that they offer female clubbers an environment in which they can challenge traditional signifiers of femininity. Even if this is still risky and problematic at times, the fact that they are able to pose a challenge in the first place speaks volumes about the changing nature of gendered relations in (sub)cultural spaces. It is also promising to see that female clubbers are moving towards being heard as well as seen, no longer prepared to accept their marginalized gendered positions. Although it must also be noted that even within the production of club spaces the inequalities found in wider society are reproduced, indicating that there is still a considerable way to go before equality of opportunity is apparent.

Women participating in club scenes are creating spaces for themselves, which are visible within the night time world of the city. A key theme that has been explored are the differences between club spaces and the implications that these have for the experiences of women who participate in them. Difference means that certain types of people congregate in particular spaces, with certain attitudes, to listen to certain types of music, use drugs in a particular way, and to interact with others within certain parameters. Difference and *attitude* underpin women's experiences of risk in relation to sexual encounters, drug use and the use of the city at night. The analysis of the different social rules or 'codes' that operate in different club spaces illuminate that important distinctions have to be made between *mainstream* and *underground* club spaces and also within these categories. The typology of *mainstreams* and *undergrounds* has been developed as an analytical tool to explore the complexity of these differences. Previous analyses of club scenes have treated *mainstream* and *underground* as homogeneous categories (Thornton 1996), but the need to differentiate between the spaces contained within these two categories has also become apparent. Therefore it is more useful to refer to *mainstreams* and *undergrounds*. The concept of *attitude* has also been developed to explore difference and the effects it has on the women involved in clubbing. It is argued that what is analysed as *attitude* was seen by female clubbers as the main defining factor in determining who belongs where. Having a right *attitude* underwrites everything else that is important to those taking part in club scenes, without which participants will be excluded. The 'right' attitude as defined by female clubbers was one that included appropriate behaviour towards women such as the absence of sexual harassment, tolerance of different sexualities and tolerance of expressions of female identities.

In order to explore the construction of femininities within club spaces a focus on how women participating in club scenes related, and were attracted, to different spaces is important. In chapter 2 it is highlighted that identities for female clubbers are not static, and that they are linked to notions of style, music, *attitude* and sexual behaviour. Female identity within club spaces was seen as fluid, so identities could be created to 'fit in' to particular scenes as appropriate. Female clubbers 'dabbled' in the different spaces available and this made *attitude* all the more relevant as it was a crucial signifier in determining who belonged where. 'Style' also placed female clubbers in different spaces, and differences in style were related to the typology of *mainstreams* and *undergrounds*. Mainstream clubs were seen as much more constricting in terms of style, with official dress codes that meant women had to conform to traditional images of femininity to gain access to these spaces. Underground spaces were seen as less conventional in terms of style and female clubbers were therefore less constricted and controlled by stylistic conventions. Many of the female clubbers presented here had started their clubbing careers on *mainstreams*, but became dissatisfied with these scenes due to the harassment of women and *attitudes* of those attending. They had then moved through the course of their clubbing careers to *undergrounds* where they felt much safer and more satisfied with the *attitudes* of others, particularly men who attended these spaces. There are a wide variety of diverse spaces for clubbing that can be divided and sub divided into categories supporting the notion that these transient groups are not (sub)cultures. There are however definite rules that operate within particular spaces regarding behaviour and attitude and unless participants adhere to these rules they are excluded. Neo tribes (Bennett 1999; Mafessoli 1996) are formed and reformed in contemporary society and membership of these tribes or (sub)cultures is not fixed or even confined to just one group. Female clubbers choose where they want to be and fit in where they feel an affinity with others.

The relationship between the experience of women as consumers and the ways in which club spaces are produced has also been explored through issues relating to DJ-ing, drug dealing and promoting. This exploration highlighted the fact that the gender inequalities of wider society are apparent within the production of club scenes. The production of subcultural spaces needs careful analysis as producers of club spaces are seen to have a crucial role (McRobbie 1994). Production is linked to *attitude* and I have concentrated on how far the position of women as producers of club spaces mirrors the experiences of female consumers in terms of their marginalization. Women promoters and DJs are a minority amongst the producers of club spaces and one explanation for the gender inequalities that are apparent is the misogyny of male operators in these spaces. Where women did carve a niche for themselves as producers they experienced problems, but faced them in different ways. The 'hegemonic masculinity' (Connell 1995) that surrounds the professions of DJ-ing and promoting only makes it harder for female producers to negotiate these social worlds. Both the spaces used for networking and the anti-social hours needed to be a success also excluded women as producers of club spaces. It was significant that when women did manage to perform functions such as DJ-ing and promoting, their experiences were embedded in the gender expectations formed in everyday life. This was apparent in the lower expectations of the technical expertise of women DJs in areas such as mixing, and in the intimidation they suffered at the hands of some male colleagues. The pressures were on them to be twice as good and work harder and in addition women are simply not taken seriously in a male dominated world of popular culture, within which it can be argued that 'outdated rock ideals' still prevail (Negus 1992).

Gender inequalities can also be observed in another aspect of production of scenes; 'drug dealing'. Just being a woman in this hidden world offended the rigid social rules of the dominant discourses of masculinity that operate throughout the negotiation of drug dealing. This book can claim some measure of uniqueness in the form of the data obtained from a female drug dealer, 'Melanie'. One of the main concerns in analysing this data was to expand the idea of risk in relation to lifestyle in drug dealing, and to explore how gender affects the level of risk associated with dealing in terms of interacting with customers, suppliers and the police. In this context gender visibility is a drawback, and to counteract this 'Melanie' rendered herself invisible by pooling her resources with an established male dealer. This helped to remove her from the aggressive culture of masculinity and threat of violence inherent in dealing. It was also a form of empowerment as she 'got one over' on the suppliers who had been cheating her financially. In this way the female drug dealer can be seen to opt out of the game of 'hipness' as theorized by Thornton (1995), a strategy which also removes her from danger. She does not mind being invisible to suppliers and customers, as she is not 'macho' in her attitudes towards being in the background. One of her main problems however was the fact that she was mistrusted by other dealers who thought she was a liability in terms of law enforcement. This meant she was seen as the marginalized 'other', as invisible, and that information was withheld by more powerful male dealers. Therefore in terms of lifestyle gender is a signifier of risk in the world of drug dealing. To be a woman and a drug dealer carries a double risk: the need to avoid the police, and also to avoid aggression and suspicion from other male dealers.

As argued in chapter 1, risk, danger and pleasure are linked in women's experiences of club spaces. Female clubbers balance the risks they take in participating in club spaces with the pleasures that they derive from this participation. It has been argued that 'rave' poses no challenges to society in terms of politics as it is based on hedonistic pleasure seeking (Miles 2000). Whilst it can be argued that using drugs, having sex and dancing are hedonistic practices safely contained within a commodified culture, there is a more oppositional potential to these clubbing practices that can be explored by taking into account gender difference. This oppositional potential is not recognized as the experience of women clubbers is ignored. Women derive pleasure not only from taking drugs and exploring their sexuality but also from their personal challenges to the stereotypical constructs of femininity. Risk is negotiated within the public and private spaces of the city, and within interactions relating to drug use and sexual encounters. Women are perceived in popular representations as indulging in risk taking behaviour when visibly being out in the city at night and using drugs. Although such behaviour can be construed as risky, any pleasures gained by women through participation in the night time economy are marginalized by discussions concerning danger. Women's access to the city is regulated by constraints on their behaviour in the public and in the private (Stanko 1990, 1997), and women encounter and need to manage risk on a daily basis, which determines their use of space. Outside spaces are seen as dangerous due to the presence of 'dangerous men' (Seabrook and Green 2000), and the experiences of female clubbers emphasize that it is the threat of male aggression and verbal abuse which affects their use of the public space of the city. While female clubbers had to negotiate 'dangerous' space, this led them to what they perceived as the safer spaces of clubbing venues themselves. The dangers that arose in city spaces were due to the attitudes of men outside clubbing spaces who taunted or harassed women, either because they did not conform to traditional feminine images or because they were seen as traditional sexual objects. Certain areas of the city were avoided by women due to the verbal abuse, and the threat of violence they encountered. In this context female friendship networks were crucial in maintaining safety when 'out and about' and women gained a sense of satisfaction and pleasure when arriving at the safer spaces of clubs, in having negotiated the risks of the city successfully.

The debate surrounding visibility, safety and risk is moved forward here, in that I highlight women's attempts to keep themselves safe and how they negotiate this aspect of risk, in relation to their participation in club spaces. Female clubbers were acutely aware of the dangers of traversing the city at night and went to great lengths to minimize risk in this aspect of their involvement in club scenes. Risk and pleasure however are not only negotiated in the public spaces of the city. Club spaces themselves are perceived to be 'safe' although the differences between the spaces used for clubbing means that 'safe' is relative to context for female clubbers. Arguments about the negotiation of risk have to be made within an understanding of the social rules (the *attitude*) that constructs different spaces. *Mainstreams* were seen as being less safe because of the different social rules that framed participation in these scenes in comparison to *undergrounds*. For women taking part in club spaces where they feel safe is a positive and pleasurable experience. A 'text of excitement' can be used to describe clubbing as a celebration of excitement and pleasure which is generated by using ecstasy and 'losing' oneself in the erotic expression of dance (Pini 1997). In spaces where women feel comfortable to indulge in such pleasure seeking behaviour, the absence of aggression from male participants is a pleasure in itself.

In contrast to the stereotypical image of passive drug users who are victims of unscrupulous men, female clubbers made decisions relating to the amount and types of drugs they used and were responsible for procuring their own supplies. Also in contrast to the view of women as passive and 'victims', the use of drugs such as ecstasy was a source of pleasure for women. The 'rushes'[1] from 'coming up' on the drug were described in ecstatic terms, as were feelings of 'being at one'[2] with friends and partners. Female clubbers were active and independent in terms of their use of drugs, and always tried to manage risks when participating in drug taking behaviour.

The view that ecstasy-based club scenes are spaces that are devoid of power struggles has also been challenged as has the idea that female clubbers are treated equally within these spaces. It is recognized that club spaces are stratified within themselves (Thornton 1995), and this is a key argument debated in this book, as female clubbers stated that some club spaces were *more* equal than other environments such as alcohol-based clubs, but that the harassment of women still occurred. It is important to note here that club spaces differ in how far the power brokering in different environments relates to sexism and sexual harassment. The impression

---

1   The 'rush' or feeling of 'coming up' on ecstasy is when the effects of the drug start to be felt. This can be an intense feeling and in some clubbers it induces nausea or vomiting.

2   Psychologically ecstasy is a empathogen-entactogen; empathogenic means the ability to communicate things to others or the ability to feel empathy towards others and entactogenic means feeling well or good with yourself and the world (Bellis, cited in Reynolds 1997 in Green 2005, 119).

that ecstasy-based club spaces promote gender and sexual equality is disputed by the analysis of different 'social rules' of club scenes. These reveal that whilst the overt harassment of women is not acceptable, such behaviour has disappeared underground, and still occurs in a much more subtle covert form. The assumption that somehow the 'battle has been won' and equality achieved in club spaces is thus questioned. However, what is positive for women participating in club spaces is that the environment is a *more* equal one than previously experienced. The pleasure clubbing on *undergrounds* affords is expressed in an implicit feminist dissatisfaction with *mainstreams*, and the forms of masculinity found within these spaces.

Drug use is not seen by female clubbers to have a significant effect on safer sexual behaviour such as condom use, as alcohol, rather than drug use produced risk-taking behaviour. It has been argued in chapter 4 that women's attitudes to condom use and safer sex in conjunction with drug use are based on levels of self-esteem and self-confidence. Within the differing club scenes the types of drugs used and the attitudes towards using them may be different, but the result in relation to sexual behaviour is not; it is not using drugs in itself that produces 'risky' behaviour in relation to sex. However, as *mainstreams* in general are likely to be more alcohol-based than *undergrounds*, it could be concluded that women in these spaces might behave in a more sexually-risky way. It can also be concluded that women gain pleasure and satisfaction from experimenting with sex and drugs. Sex when mixed with drugs was described as an intense, pleasurable experience that female clubbers enjoyed, despite the risks that sometimes have to be negotiated. Unlike the homogeneous approach to 'risk', the issues raised here highlight a sliding scale of risk, related to *attitude*, which is dependent on where women chose to participate within club scenes.

This analysis of a sliding scale of risk can also be applied to the risk of exploring different sexualities. The significance of *attitude* in relation to tolerance of different sexualities has been emphasized in chapter 5. Club scenes are highly charged sexualized spaces where sexuality is constantly negotiated as an aspect of *attitude*. However, different scenes are more or less tolerant of behaviour where heteronormative rules of sexuality are challenged. Female clubbers enjoyed having the freedom to explore different aspects of their sexualities within club spaces that allowed them to do so in a 'safe' way and feeling that they had a right to experiment was pleasurable in itself. Women attending *undergrounds* are expected to be open-minded, and tolerant of differences between themselves and others. However, this tolerance was not perceived as being apparent in *mainstream* clubs, and female clubbers did not feel safe in expressing differing sexualities in these spaces. The right of others to be experimental or different was recognized by female clubbers, but it was highlighted that in being experimental with sexualities there were inherent dangers. It was not other women who were seen as restricting same-sex affection, but some of the men attending club nights, and women feared censure and aggression from men not women within club spaces. This again is linked to the differences in club spaces as some mainstream clubs were seen as a definite 'no-go area' for expressing sexual feelings for other women, whilst some more underground nights were seen as safer. However even in perceived safer underground spaces, tolerance was not as apparent as it was expected to be.

One of the main reasons why some club spaces were regarded as safer for women was the lack of emphasis on alcohol consumption. However, female clubbers referred to the developing bar scene, comprised of bar spaces with late licences to sell alcohol that also included DJs and dance floor spaces. These types of spaces are a 'halfway house' between a pub and a club, with the consumption of alcohol being more central to the experience, compared with ecstasy based club spaces. This raises interesting questions regarding women's use of these late licensed bars. This could be viewed as a positive development as they could be seen as a less male-orientated space than traditional pubs. However, female clubbers stated that alcohol produced more risky behaviour both in others and in themselves. It is the consumption of alcohol within club spaces that makes the use of drugs and the pursuit of pleasure more risky, as it is a contradiction of the early 'luved up' atmosphere. Therefore alcohol use and the licensing of club spaces can be seen as moving the atmosphere away from the earlier alcohol-free 'rave' scene towards a more risky use of spaces.[3]

The nature of club scenes is that they are diverse, dynamic (sub)cultures, evident for example, in the development of drug- and alcohol-free raves in the US (see Smalley 2003), and it is these differences in their nature that produces a wealth of experiences not just for female clubbers, but for all who participate in and do research into club spaces. When I originally started researching gendered experiences and clubbing, I wanted to hear that these fantastical new spaces and places fuelled by ecstasy pushed the boundaries of gendered power relationships and the tensions inherent within them. That they offered women places to be free, have fun, use drugs and have sex without being abused, harassed or judged. Imagine my disappointment when female clubbers stated that club spaces were 'just the same' as other places in the city, that harassment was still apparent if covert, and even *incorporated* in to the social rules of club spaces. However in amongst the sexism, the intrusions, the controls and constraints on fun-loving, pleasure-seeking women there are new ways of negotiating tensions and conflicts. These have been discussed throughout this book by female clubbers who have found places where they are on a *more* equal footing with their male counterparts. May these relationships continue to evolve and change and may we get there in the end.

---

3   This change in consumption of alcohol can also be related to changes in drug use that were inferred by female clubbers. Bad quality ecstasy led to higher levels of cocaine use, and drugs cocktails such as acid and speed, speed and ecstasy, cocaine and ecstasy, mixed with alcohol to enhance the effect.

Bibliography

Barnes, R. et al. (1991), *Mods!* (London: Plexus Publishing Limited).

Beck, U. (1992), *Risk Society: Towards a New Modernity* (London: Sage).

Bell, D. and Valentine, G. (1995), *Mapping Desires: Geographies of Sexualities* (London: Routledge).

Bellis, M. and Kilfoyle, M. (1998), *Club Health: The Health of the Clubbing Nation* (Liverpool: Print House).

Bennett, A. (1999), 'Subcultures or Neo Tribes? Rethinking the Relationship between Youth, Style and Musical Taste', *Sociology* 33: 3, 599–617.

Brown, S. (1998), *Understanding Youth and Crime: Listening to Youth* (Buckingham: Open University Press).

Budgeon, S. (1998), '"I'll Tell You What I Really Really Want": Girl Power and Self-Identity in Britain', in Sherrie Inness (ed.) (1998), *Millennium Girls: Today's Girls and the World* (Lanham: Rowman and Littlefield Publishers Inc.).

Butler, J. (1990), *Gender Trouble* (London: Routledge).

Calcutt, A. (1998), *Arrested Development: Popular Culture and the Erosion of Adulthood* (London: Cassell).

Carlen, P. and Christina, D. (eds) (1985), *Criminal Women: Autobiographical Accounts* (Oxford: Polity Press).

Carrington, B. and Wilson, B. (2004), 'Dance Nations: Rethinking Youth Subcultural Theory', in Andy Bennett and Keith Kahn-Harris (eds) (2004), *After Subculture: Critical Studies in Contemporary Youth Culture* (Basingstoke: Palgrave Macmillan).

Chan, W. and Rigakos, G. (2002), 'Risk, Crime and Gender', *British Journal of Criminology* 42: 4 743–61.

Collin, M. (1997), *Altered State: The Story of Ecstasy Culture and Acid House* (London: Serpents Tail).

Connell, R. (1995), *Masculinities* (New South Wales: Allen and Unwin).

Davies, P. (1999), 'Women Crime and an Informal Economy: Female Offending and Crime for Gain', http://www.brtisoccrim.org/bccsp/vol102/01DAVIEHTM, accessed 4 December 2003.

Dean, M. (1999), 'Risk Calculable and Incalculable', in Deborah Lupton (ed.) (1999), *Risk and Sociocultural Theory New Directions and Perspectives* (Cambridge: Cambridge University Press).

Denton, B. and O'Malley, P. (1999), 'Gender, Trust and Business: Women Drug Dealers in the Illicit Economy', *British Journal of Criminology* 39: 4, 513–30.

Ettorre, E. (1992), *Women and Substance Use* (Basingstoke: Macmillan Press Ltd).

Featherstone, M. (1990), *Global Culture: Nationalism, Globalization and Modernity* (London: Sage in association with Theory, Culture and Society).

Ferrell, J. and Sanders, C. (eds) (1995), *Cultural Criminology* (Boston: Northeastern University Press).

Fielding, N. (1993), 'Ethnography', in Nigel Gilbert (ed.) (1993), *Researching Social Life* (London: Sage).

Finch, J. (1993), 'It's Great to Have Someone to Talk to: The Ethics of Interviewing Women', in Martyn Hammersley (ed.) (1993), *Social Research: Philosophy, Politics and Practice* (London: Sage).

Fox, N. (1999), 'Postmodern Reflections on "Risk", "Hazards" and Life Choices', in Deborah Lupton (ed.) (1999), *Risk and Sociocultural Theory New Directions and Perspectives* (Cambridge: Cambridge University Press).

Furlong, A. and Cartmel, F. (1997), *Young People and Social Change* (Buckingham: Open University Press).

Gelsthorpe, L. (1989), *Sexism and the Female Offender: An Organisational Analysis* (Aldershot: Gower).

Giddens, A. (1991), *The Consequences of Modernity* (Cambridge: Polity).

Green, E. and Hebron, S. (1990), *Women's Leisure, What Leisure?* (Basingstoke: Macmillan Education).

Gore, G. (1997), 'The Beat Goes on: Trance, Dance and Tribalism in Rave Culture?', in Helen Thomas (ed.) (1997), *Dance in the City* (Basingstoke: Macmillan Press Ltd).

Hall, S. et al. (1975), 'Subcultures, Cultures and Class', in Ken Gelder and Sarah Thornton (eds) (1997), *The Subcultures Reader* (London: Routledge).

Harris, A. (2004), *Future Girl: Young Women in the 21st Century* (London: Routledge).

Haslam, D. (1999), *Manchester, England: The Story of the Pop Cult City* (London: Fourth Estate).

Haslam, D. (2002), 'The Rise of DJ Culture', in Jared Green (ed.) (2005), *Dance and Rave Culture* (Detroit: Greenhaven Press).

Hebdige, D. (1979), *Subcultures and the Meaning of Style* (London: Methuen).

Henderson, S. (1993), 'Luved Up and De-elited: Responses to Drug Use in the Second Decade', in Peter Aggleton et al. (eds) (1993), *AIDS: Facing the Second Decade* (London: Falmer Press).

Henderson, S. (1996), 'E Types and Dance Divas', in Tim Rhodes and Richard Hartnoll (eds) (1996), *AIDS, Drugs and Prevention: Perspectives on Individual and Community Action* (London: Routledge).

Hey, V. (1997), *The Company She Keeps* (Buckingham: Open University Press).

Hey, V. (1986), *Patriarchy and Pub Culture* (London: Women's Press).

Hobbs, D. et al. (2003), *Bouncers: Violence and Governance in the Night Time Economy* (Oxford: Oxford University Press).

Holland, J. et al. (1999), 'Feminist Methodology and Young People's Sexuality', in Peter Aggleton et al. (eds) (1999), *Culture, Society and Sexuality: A Reader* (London: UCL Press).

Holland, J. (1992), *Pressured Pleasure: Young Women and the Negotiation of Sexual Boundaries* (London: Tufnell Press WRAP paper series 7).

Hunt, G. and Evans, K. (2003), 'Dancing and Drugs: A Cross National Perspective', *Contemporary Drug Problems* 30: 4, 779–815.

Katz, J. (1988), *The Seductions of Crime* (US: Harper Collins).

Khon, M. (1992), *Dope Girls: The Birth of the British Drug Underground* (London: Lawrence and Wishart).

Laurie, N. et al. (1999), *Geographies of New Femininities* (Essex: Pearsons Education Ltd).

Lees, S. (1993), *Sugar and Spice: Sexuality and Adolescent Girls* (London: Penguin).

Lees, S. (1997), *Ruling Passions: Sexual Violence, Reputations and the Law* (Buckingham: Open University Press).

Leonard, M. (1997), 'Rebel Girl You are the Queen of my World, Feminism, "Subculture" and Grrrl Power', in Sheila Whiteley (ed.) (1997), *Sexing the Groove* (London: Routledge).

Logan, B. (1998), 'So You Want to be a DJ? Let's See Your Legs', *The Guardian*, July 11th 1998.

Lovatt, A. (1996), 'The Ecstasy of Urban Regeneration: Regulation of the Night Time Economy in the Transition to a Post-Fordist City', in Justin O'Connor and Derek Wynne (eds) (1996), *From the Margins to the Centre: Cultural Production and Consumption in the Post Industrial City* (Aldershot: Arena).

Lupton, D. (ed.) (1999), *Risk and Sociocultural Theory: New Directions and Perspectives* (Cambridge: Cambridge University Press).

Lyotard, J. (1984), *The Postmodern Condition* (Manchester: Manchester University Press).

Maffesoli, M. (1996), *The Time of the Tribes: The Decline of Individualism in Mass Society* (London: Sage).

Malbon, B. (1998), 'Clubbing: Consumption, Identity and the Spatial Practices of Every-night Life', in Tracey Skelton and Gill Valentine (eds) (1998), *Cool Places: Geographies of Youth Cultures* (London: Routledge).

Massey, D. (1994), *Space, Place and Gender* (Cambridge: Polity Press).

McRobbie, A. and Garber, J. (1975), 'Girls and Subcultures', in Ken Gelder and Sarah Thornton (eds) (1997), *The Subcultures Reader* (London: Routledge).

McRobbie, A. (1994), 'Shut Up and Dance: Youth Culture and Changing Modes of Femininity', in Angela McRobbie (ed.) (1994), *Post Modernism and Popular Culture* (London: Routledge).

Meesham, F. et al. (2000), *Dancing on Drugs Risk Health and Hedonism in the British Club Scene* (London: Free Association Press).

Miles, C. (1997), *A Gendered Sense of Place* (Manchester: Manchester Metropolitan University, Institute for Popular Culture).

Miles, S. (2000), *Youth Lifestyles in a Changing World* (Buckingham: Open University Press).

Milestone, K. and Richards, N. (1999), 'What Difference Does it Make? Women's Pop Cultural Production and Consumption in Manchester', unpublished conference paper (Manchester: Manchester Institute for Popular Culture).

Miller, T. (1991), *The Hippies and American Values* (Knoxville: University of Tennessee Press).

Muggleton, D. (2000), *Inside Subculture: The Postmodern Meaning of Style* (Oxford: Berg).

Naffine, N. (1996), *Feminism and Criminology* (Cambridge: Polity Press).

Negus, K. (1992), *Producing Pop: Culture and Conflict in the Popular Music Industry* (London: E.Arnold).

Oakly, A. (1985), *The Sociology of Housework* (Oxford: Basil Blackwell).

Pini, M. (1997), 'Women and the Early British Rave Scene', in Angela McRobbie (ed.) (1997), *Back to Reality? Social Experience and Cultural Studies* (Manchester: Manchester University Press).

Pini, M. (2001), *Club Cultures and Female Subjectivity: The Move from Home to House* (Basingstoke: Palgrave).

Redhead, S. (1993), 'The Politics of Ecstasy', in Steve Redhead (ed.) (1993), *Rave Off: Politics and Deviance in Contemporary Youth Culture* (Aldershot: Ashgate).

Richard, B. and Kruger, H. (1998), 'Ravers' Paradise? German Youth Cultures in the 1990s', in Tracey Skelton and Gill Valentine (eds) (1998), *Cool Places: Geographies of Youth Cultures* (London: Routledge).

Reitveld, H. (1998), *This is Our House: House Music, Cultural Spaces and Technologies* (Aldershot: Ashgate).

Reynolds, S. (1997), 'Rave Culture: Living Dream or Living Death?', in Jared Green (ed.) (2005), *Dance and Rave Culture* (Detroit: Greenhaven Press).

Rosenbaum, M. (1981), *Women on Heroin* (New Jersey: Rutgers).

Ryan, J. (1994), 'Women Modernity and the City', *Theory Culture and Society* 11: 4, 35–63.

Ryan, J. and Fitzpatrick, H. (1996), 'The Space that Difference Makes: Negotiation and Urban Identities through Consumption Practices', in Justin O'Connor and Derek Wynne (eds) (1996), *From the Margins to the Centre: Cultural Production and Consumption in the Post Industrial City* (Aldershot: Arena).

Sanders, B. (2005,) 'In the Club: Ecstasy Use and Supply in a London Nightclub', *Sociology* 39: 2, 241–258.

Saunders, N. (1997), *Ecstasy Reconsidered* (Exeter: Nicholas Saunders,).

Seabrook, T. and Green, E. (2000), 'Streetwise or Safe: Young Women Negotiating Time and Space', unpublished conference paper (Manchester: Cultural Change and Urban Contexts, 8th–10th September).

Skelton, T. and Valentine, G. (eds) (1998), *Cool Places: Geographies of Youth Cultures* (London: Routledge).

Skidmore, D. and Hayter, E. (2000), 'Risk and Sex: Ego-centricity and Sexual Behaviour in Young Adults', *Health, Risk and Society* 2: 1, 23–31.

Smalley, S. (2003), 'The New Age of Rave', in Jared Green (ed.) (2005), *Dance and Rave Culture* (Detroit: Greenhaven Press).

Stanko, E. (1990), *Everyday Violence: How Women and Men Experience Sexual and Physical Danger* (London: Pandora).

Stanko, E. (1997), 'Warnings to Women: Police Advice and Women's Safety in Britain', in Susan Miller (ed.) (1997), *Crime, Control and Women: Feminist Implications of Criminal Justice Policy* (London: Sage).

Straw, W. (1997) 'Sizing Up Record Collections: Gender and Connoisseurship in Rock Music Culture', in Sheila Whiteley (ed.) (1997), *Sexing the Groove* (London: Routledge).

Taylor, I. et al. (1996), *A Tale of Two Cities: Global Change, Local Feeling and Everyday Life in the North of England* (London: Routledge).

Thornton, S. (1995), *Club Cultures* (Cambridge: Polity Press).

Thornton, S. and Gelder, K. (eds) (1997), *The Subcultures Reader* (London: Routledge).

Valentine, G. (1996), '(Re) Negotiating the "Heterosexual Street" Lesbian Productions of Space', in Nancy Duncan (ed.) (1996), *Body Space* (London: Routledge).

Williamson, K. (1997), *Drugs and the Party Line* (Edinburgh: Rebel Inc.).

Willis, P. (1977), 'Culture, Institution, Differentiation', in Ken Gelder and Sarah Thornton (eds) (1997), *The Subcultures Reader* (London: Routledge).

Wilson, E. (1991), *The Sphinx in the City: Urban Life, the Control of Disorder and Women* (London: Virago).

Index